Mastering React 19: The Ultimate Guide to Modern Web Development

Matt P. Handy

TABLE OF CONTENTS
CONTENTS

INTRODUCTION

Welcome to **Mastering React 19: The Ultimate Guide to Modern Web Development**! If you're here, chances are you're excited about learning **React 19—** the latest and most advanced version of the world's most popular frontend framework. Whether you're a **beginner looking to break into web development** or an **experienced developer aiming to level up**, this book is designed to **guide you from the fundamentals to expert-level techniques**.

Why React 19?

React has been at the heart of modern web development for nearly a decade. It powers **millions of websites and applications**, from small personal projects to enterprise-scale platforms used by companies like **Meta, Airbnb, Netflix, and Uber**.

A Brief History of React

React was first introduced by **Meta (formerly Facebook)** in 2013 to solve a major problem: **building fast, interactive, and scalable user interfaces**. Since then, it has evolved significantly, with every version bringing new improvements. **React 19 is the most refined, performant, and developer-friendly version to date.**

So, what makes React 19 special?

New and Improved Features in React 19

React 19 introduces several cutting-edge features that make development **faster, easier, and more efficient**:

✅ **Compiler Optimizations** – Automatic performance improvements with less manual tweaking.
✅ **Improved React Server Components** – Faster data fetching and rendering on the server.
✅ **Better Suspense Handling** – Simplifies how we handle asynchronous UI updates.

☑ **Streamlined Hooks API** – More powerful yet easier to use than before.
☑ **Enhanced Developer Experience** – Faster refresh, improved error handling, and better debugging tools.

These enhancements mean you can build **lightning-fast, scalable, and maintainable applications** with less effort than ever before.

Who This Book Is For

This book is for **anyone who wants to master React 19**, whether you're:

👤 **A beginner** who wants a structured path to learn React from scratch.
✏️ **An intermediate developer** aiming to deepen your understanding of React's internals.
📱 **A professional developer** looking to stay ahead of the curve with React 19's latest features.

What You'll Learn

- **How React works under the hood**—understanding the Virtual DOM, reconciliation, and rendering.
- **Building reusable components and managing state efficiently** using the latest best practices.
- **Optimizing performance** with advanced React patterns and hooks.
- **Handling API requests and data fetching** with tools like React Query.
- **Mastering modern React Router and handling complex UI navigation.**
- **Testing, deploying, and scaling real-world React applications.**

By the end of this book, you'll have **the skills and confidence** to build production-ready applications **like a pro**.

Prerequisites and Setup

Before we dive in, let's make sure you have **everything you need** to get started.

What You Should Know

While this book is designed to be **accessible to all skill levels**, it helps if you have **some familiarity with JavaScript and web development basics**. If you're new to JavaScript, consider brushing up on:

- **ES6+ JavaScript features** (like arrow functions, template literals, and destructuring).
- **Basic HTML & CSS** (React handles the UI, but styling matters too!).
- **How functions and objects work** in JavaScript.

If you don't feel comfortable with these topics, don't worry—I'll explain key concepts along the way, and you can always refer to JavaScript resources online.

Setting Up Your Development Environment

Before writing any React 19 code, we need to set up our development environment properly. Here's what you'll need:

1. Install Node.js and npm

React relies on **Node.js** for package management and running development tools. To install it:

1. Go to nodejs.org and download the **latest LTS version**.
2. Install it following the instructions for your operating system.
3. Open a terminal and verify the installation:

```
node -v
npm -v
```

If you see version numbers, you're good to go!

2. Install a Code Editor (VS Code Recommended)

For the best development experience, I recommend **Visual Studio Code (VS Code)**. It's lightweight, powerful, and has great support for React development.

- Download it from code.visualstudio.com.
- Install useful extensions:
    - **ES7+ React/Redux Snippets** (for quick React boilerplate).
    - **Prettier** (for automatic code formatting).

o **React Developer Tools** (for debugging React apps).

3. Create Your First React 19 Project

React has multiple ways to start a project, but the most modern and fastest way is using **Vite**. Let's set up a new React 19 app:

1. Open your terminal and run:

```
npm create vite@latest my-react-app --template react
cd my-react-app
npm install
npm run dev
```

2. Open your browser and go to `http://localhost:5173/`—you should see your React app running! 🎉

What's Next?

Now that your development environment is set up, you're ready to dive into **Chapter 1**, where we'll explore React 19's core concepts and start building our first components.

Are you ready? Let's get started! 🚀

CHAPTER 1: GETTING STARTED WITH REACT 19

Welcome to **React 19!** If you're new to React or coming from an earlier version, this chapter will introduce you to **the core concepts** that make React such a powerful tool for building modern web applications.

By the end of this chapter, you'll:
- ☑ Understand **what React is and how it works under the hood**.
- ☑ Set up a **React 19 project** using the latest tools.
- ☑ Learn about **JSX and how React renders elements**.
- ☑ Build your **first functional components** and use props to pass data.

Let's get started! 🚀

1.1 UNDERSTANDING REACT AND ITS CORE CONCEPTS

React has become the **gold standard** for modern web development, and for good reason. It offers an intuitive, flexible approach to building **fast, interactive user interfaces**. But before diving into coding, it's important to understand **why React exists, how it works, and what makes it so powerful**.

What is React?

At its core, **React is a JavaScript library for building user interfaces**. Unlike traditional web development, where you manipulate the DOM manually, React **automates UI updates efficiently** by using a **component-based architecture** and a **Virtual DOM**.

Think of React as **the engine behind dynamic, scalable web applications**—from social media platforms like **Facebook and Instagram** to e-commerce sites and productivity tools.

One of the key reasons React gained popularity is that it **solves a real problem**: managing complex UI updates. Instead of writing **imperative** code that manually modifies the DOM, React allows developers to write **declarative** code—describing the UI **as a function of state**. This makes applications **predictable, maintainable, and scalable**.

How React Works: The Virtual DOM Advantage

One of React's most innovative features is the **Virtual DOM (VDOM)**.

Traditionally, web pages rely on the **Real DOM**, where every UI update requires modifying the actual HTML structure. The problem? **The Real DOM is slow**. Each change triggers re-rendering, layout recalculations, and repainting, which can cause performance issues, especially in large applications.

React's **Virtual DOM acts as a lightweight copy of the Real DOM**. Here's how it works:

1. When a component's state changes, React **creates a new Virtual DOM**.
2. It **compares** this new Virtual DOM with the previous one using a process called **Reconciliation**.
3. It **updates only the changed parts** of the Real DOM—avoiding unnecessary re-renders.

This makes React applications incredibly **fast and efficient**. Instead of updating everything, React **smartly updates just what's needed**.

Imagine a to-do list app: Instead of reloading the entire list when you add a new task, React updates only the new item. This is why React feels **snappy and responsive** compared to older JavaScript frameworks.

React's Declarative Approach vs. Traditional Imperative Programming

React's **declarative nature** is another game-changer.

In **imperative programming** (like jQuery or vanilla JavaScript), you write step-by-step instructions to modify the UI:

js

10

```
const button = document.querySelector("#myButton");
button.addEventListener("click", function() {
  button.textContent = "Clicked!";
});
```

With React, you simply **describe what the UI should look like**, and React takes care of updating it:

```jsx
function MyButton() {
  const [clicked, setClicked] = React.useState(false);

  return (
    <button onClick={() => setClicked(true)}>
      {clicked ? "Clicked!" : "Click me"}
    </button>
  );
}
```

This **removes complexity** and makes the UI **more predictable**—React ensures your UI **always reflects the latest state**.

The Power of Components: Building Blocks of React

React is **component-based**, meaning your UI is broken into **reusable, self-contained units**.

For example, a **social media post** can be a component:

- The **Post component** contains text, images, and user info.
- The **LikeButton component** handles likes.
- The **Comment component** displays and manages comments.

Each component **manages its own logic and state**, making it easier to **build, test, and scale applications**.

Compare this to older web development, where HTML, CSS, and JavaScript were often **intertwined and hard to manage**. React's component model **brings structure and reusability** to UI development.

State and Props: Managing Data in React

Two key concepts in React are **State and Props**.

- **State** is used **inside a component** to store dynamic data. It changes over time (e.g., a user's input or a counter).
- **Props** allow **data to be passed from a parent to a child component**, making components reusable.

Let's illustrate this with a simple example:

```jsx
function Greeting(props) {
  return <h1>Hello, {props.name}!</h1>;
}

function App() {
  return (
    <div>
      <Greeting name="Alice" />
      <Greeting name="Bob" />
    </div>
  );
}
```

Here, the **Greeting component** receives a **name prop** and displays it. The **App component** renders it twice, with different values.

On the other hand, **state** is used when a component needs to track **changes over time**:

```jsx
function Counter() {
  const [count, setCount] = React.useState(0);

  return (
    <div>
      <p>Count: {count}</p>
      <button onClick={() => setCount(count +
1)}>Increment</button>
    </div>
  );
}
```

Here, React **remembers the count value**, and each time the button is clicked, it updates the UI automatically.

Why React? The Competitive Edge

React's popularity isn't just about **ease of use**—it offers real advantages over other frameworks like **Vue and Angular**.

1. **Performance** – The Virtual DOM ensures fast updates.
2. **Flexibility** – React can be used for **web apps, mobile apps (React Native), and even VR (React VR)**.
3. **Strong Ecosystem** – Rich libraries and tools, from Redux to Next.js.
4. **Large Community & Job Market** – Thousands of React jobs and strong support from Meta.

React also **works seamlessly with modern development tools** like **TypeScript, Vite, and Tailwind CSS**, making it ideal for production-grade applications.

Final Thoughts

React's approach to UI development is **game-changing**. By leveraging the **Virtual DOM, declarative programming, and component-based architecture**, it simplifies building complex, interactive applications.

1.2 SETTING UP A REACT 19 PROJECT

Getting started with React 19 is easier than ever, thanks to modern tools that streamline the development process. In this chapter, we'll walk through setting up a React project using **Vite**, a faster and more efficient alternative to Create React App. We'll also explore the project structure, key files, and best practices to ensure a smooth development experience.

Why Vite Instead of Create React App?

For years, developers relied on **Create React App (CRA)** to scaffold React projects. While it worked well, it had some drawbacks—**slow startup times, long build processes, and unnecessary bloat**. Enter **Vite**.

Vite (French for "fast") significantly improves performance by:

- **Using native ES modules**, which eliminate slow bundling during development.
- **Hot Module Replacement (HMR)**, allowing instant updates without a full page reload.
- **Minimal configuration**, making it ideal for modern React projects.

Switching to Vite means **faster startup times, better performance, and a more enjoyable development experience**.

Installing Node.js and npm

Before creating a React project, ensure you have **Node.js** installed. React relies on **npm (Node Package Manager)** to manage dependencies.

To check if Node.js is installed, open a terminal and run:

```sh
node -v
```
```sh
npm -v
```

If these commands return version numbers, you're good to go. Otherwise, download and install the latest **LTS version** from nodejs.org.

Creating a React 19 Project with Vite

Once Node.js is set up, creating a React project is straightforward. Open your terminal and run:

```sh
npm create vite@latest my-react-app --template react
```

This command does a few things:

- It initializes a new React project inside the `my-react-app` directory.
- It sets up Vite as the build tool.
- It preconfigures everything for a modern development workflow.

Once the setup completes, navigate into the project directory:

```sh
cd my-react-app
```

Install dependencies:

```sh
npm install
```

Finally, start the development server:

```sh
npm run dev
```

You'll see output similar to this:

```
VITE v4.0.0  ready in 200ms
→ Local: http://localhost:5173/
```

Open the link in your browser, and you'll see your first React 19 app running!

Understanding the Project Structure

A fresh Vite-powered React project contains the following structure:

```
my-react-app/
|── src/
|    ├── App.jsx        # Main component
|    ├── main.jsx       # Renders App component
|    ├── index.css      # Global styles
|── public/
|── package.json        # Manages dependencies
```

```
|── vite.config.js    # Vite configuration
```

The `src/` folder is where all React code lives. Key files include:

- **App.jsx** – This is the main component that renders the UI.
- **main.jsx** – The entry point that renders `<App />` inside the `#root` div.
- **index.css** – A global stylesheet for styling.

The **public/** folder contains static assets like images and icons.

First Look at React 19's Entry Point

Let's examine **main.jsx**, where the app begins execution:

```jsx
import React from "react";
import ReactDOM from "react-dom/client";
import App from "./App.jsx";

ReactDOM.createRoot(document.getElementById("root")).render(<App
/>);
```

A few key takeaways:

- **ReactDOM.createRoot()** is the new way to initialize React in React 18+. It enables **concurrent rendering**, improving performance.
- It targets an HTML element (`id="root"`) to inject the entire React application.

This means React doesn't modify the whole page—it dynamically updates only necessary parts.

Updating App.jsx: Your First Component

Now, let's modify `App.jsx` to display a simple welcome message:

```jsx
function App() {
  return (
```

```
    <div>
      <h1>Welcome to React 19!</h1>
      <p>Let's build something amazing.</p>
    </div>
  );
}

export default App;
```

Here's what's happening:

- **App is a functional component**, which returns JSX (JavaScript + XML).
- It contains a simple `<h1>` and `<p>` inside a `<div>`.
- React dynamically injects this component into the `#root` div in `index.html`.

If you save and refresh the browser, you'll see your new message.

Why This Setup Matters

Setting up a React project properly is **crucial for long-term maintainability**. With Vite, you get:

- **Instant startup times** (even in large projects).
- **Out-of-the-box HMR** (real-time updates while coding).
- **Optimized builds** with minimal configuration.

It also lays the groundwork for **state management, component structuring, and routing**, which we'll cover in later chapters.

1.3 JSX AND RENDERING ELEMENTS

JSX is at the heart of React. It looks like HTML but is actually a **syntax extension for JavaScript**. If you've ever written React code, you've already used JSX, even if you didn't realize it. But what makes JSX so powerful, and how does React use it to efficiently render elements? Let's explore.

What is JSX?

JSX stands for **JavaScript XML**, and it allows us to write HTML-like syntax directly inside JavaScript. It makes UI code more **readable and expressive** while keeping logic and structure in the same place.

Here's a simple JSX example:

```jsx
const element = <h1>Hello, React!</h1>;
```

This looks like regular HTML, but it's actually **JavaScript under the hood**. The browser doesn't understand JSX directly, so React **transforms it into pure JavaScript** before rendering it.

Without JSX, the same code would look like this:

```js
const element = React.createElement("h1", null, "Hello, React!");
```

Which one looks cleaner? JSX is **not required** to write React, but it makes code much easier to understand and maintain.

How JSX Works Under the Hood

React **compiles JSX into JavaScript objects** using `React.createElement()`. Each element becomes a **React element**, a lightweight representation of what should appear in the UI.

For example, this JSX:

```jsx
const element = <h1 className="greeting">Hello, React!</h1>;
```

Compiles into this:

```js
const element = React.createElement("h1", { className: "greeting" }, "Hello, React!");
```

React elements are **immutable**—once created, they cannot be changed. Instead, React **creates a new element and updates only the necessary parts** of the UI. This is what makes React **efficient**.

Embedding Expressions in JSX

JSX isn't just for static content; it allows embedding **JavaScript expressions** using {}. This is powerful because it lets us dynamically render content based on logic.

For example:

```jsx
const name = "Alice";
const element = <h1>Hello, {name}!</h1>;
```

Inside {}, we can include:

- **Variables** ({name})
- **Functions** ({formatDate(date)})
- **Expressions** ({2 + 2})
- **Ternary operators** ({isLoggedIn ? "Welcome" : "Please log in"})

However, JSX does not support **statements** like if or for. Those should be handled outside the JSX block.

JSX and Attributes

JSX attributes work similarly to HTML, but with some key differences:

- **class becomes className** (since class is a reserved JavaScript keyword).
- **style accepts an object** instead of a string.

Example:

```jsx
const element = <h1 className="title" style={{ color: "blue", fontSize: "24px" }}>Hello, React!</h1>;
```

Each style property is written in **camelCase**, and the values are wrapped in an object.

Rendering Elements in the DOM

React elements describe what should appear on the screen, but they don't actually render themselves. That's where **ReactDOM** comes in.

In a standard React app, the entry point file (e.g., `main.jsx`) looks like this:

```jsx
import React from "react";
import ReactDOM from "react-dom/client";
import App from "./App.jsx";

ReactDOM.createRoot(document.getElementById("root")).render(<App
/>);
```

Here's what happens:

1. `document.getElementById("root")` selects the root **DOM node** where React will render everything.
2. `ReactDOM.createRoot()` sets up React's **concurrent rendering** capabilities.
3. `.render(<App />)` tells React to render the `<App />` component inside the root.

If we were rendering a simple element instead of a component, it would look like this:

```jsx
const element = <h1>Hello, React 19!</h1>;
ReactDOM.createRoot(document.getElementById("root")).render(element
);
```

Updating the UI: React's Efficient Rendering

Unlike traditional JavaScript frameworks, React doesn't re-render the entire UI when something changes. Instead, it uses the **Virtual DOM** to determine the **smallest possible updates**.

Consider this counter component:

```jsx
function Counter() {
  const [count, setCount] = React.useState(0);

  return (
    <div>
      <p>Count: {count}</p>
      <button onClick={() => setCount(count +
1)}>Increment</button>
    </div>
  );
}
```

Each time the button is clicked, React:

1. **Creates a new Virtual DOM tree** with the updated count.
2. **Compares it to the previous tree** using a process called **Reconciliation**.
3. **Updates only the necessary part of the Real DOM**, keeping performance high.

This is why React apps feel **fast and responsive**.

JSX Best Practices

- **Keep JSX readable** – Break long JSX into multiple lines using parentheses:

```jsx
const element = (
  <div>
    <h1>Title</h1>
    <p>Subtitle</p>
  </div>
);
```

- **Use fragments (<>...</>) instead of unnecessary <div>s:**

```jsx
function MyComponent() {
  return (
    <>
```

```jsx
    <h1>Heading</h1>
      <p>Paragraph</p>
    </>
  );
}
```

- **Use self-closing tags when possible**:

```jsx
<img src="logo.png" alt="Logo" />
```

These small improvements make JSX **more readable and maintainable**.

1.4 FUNCTIONAL COMPONENTS AND PROPS

React 19 encourages **functional components** over class components.

What Are Functional Components?

A **functional component** is a simple JavaScript function that **returns JSX**.

```jsx
function Welcome() {
  return <h1>Hello, React 19!</h1>;
}
```

These are:
- ☑ **Easier to write and read**
- ☑ **More performant**
- ☑ **Support React Hooks**

Using Props to Pass Data

Props (short for "properties") allow you to **pass data** between components.

Example: Passing Props

```jsx
function Welcome(props) {
  return <h1>Hello, {props.name}!</h1>;
```

```
}

function App() {
  return (
    <div>
      <Welcome name="Alice" />
      <Welcome name="Bob" />
    </div>
  );
}

export default App;
```

Here's what happens:

- The **App component** renders `<Welcome />` twice.
- Each time, it passes a **different name** as a prop.
- The **Welcome component receives the prop** and displays dynamic text.

Destructuring Props (Cleaner Code!)

A cleaner way to write this:

```jsx
jsx

function Welcome({ name }) {
  return <h1>Hello, {name}!</h1>;
}
```

Much better!

What's Next?

Congratulations! 🎉 You've learned:

✅ What React is and how it works.
✅ How to set up a React 19 project.
✅ JSX fundamentals and rendering elements.
✅ Functional components and passing props.

In **Chapter 2**, we'll explore **React state, lifecycle, and hooks** to make our apps **interactive and dynamic**.

Ready? Let's dive in! 🚀

CHAPTER 2: STATE AND LIFECYCLE IN REACT 19

Now that we have a solid foundation on React components and props, it's time to take things up a notch by introducing the concepts of state and lifecycle. These two concepts are really going to be the meat of how we write most of our react applications going forward. State makes our components interactive, events allow user interaction, and React Hooks give us control of a component's lifecycle.

2.1 UNDERSTANDING STATE AND EVENTS: A DEEP DIVE

State and events are the dynamic duo that brings interactivity to our React applications. Without them, our components would remain static, displaying the same information without responding to user actions or data changes. Think of state as the component's internal memory and events as its way of interacting with the world.

State: The Component's Memory

In essence, **state** is a JavaScript object that holds data within a component. This data can be anything from user input, to whether a button is toggled, or a list of items fetched from an API. What makes state special is its ability to trigger UI updates when its values change. Unlike props, which are immutable data passed down from parent components, state is mutable and managed by the component itself.

Let's explore this with a basic example. We'll create a simple button that increments a counter each time it's clicked.

```
import React, { useState } from 'react';

function Counter() {
  // Initialize state with a counter that starts at 0
  const [count, setCount] = useState(0);

  return (
    <div>
      <p>Count: {count}</p>
      <button>Increment</button>
    </div>
```

```
  );
}
export default Counter;
```

Right now, you will see that if you click on the button, nothing happens. Let's make this interactive by introducing events.

Events: Handling User Interactions

Events in React allow our components to respond to user interactions like clicks, form submissions, mouse movements, and so on. React events are syntactically similar to HTML events (e.g., onclick becomes onClick in React), but are handled internally using a synthetic event system.

To make our counter work, we need to listen for the click event on our button. To do this, we'll add an event handler to the button element. Let's start by adding a function to handle the event, but not yet using it:

```
import React, { useState } from 'react';

function Counter() {
  const [count, setCount] = useState(0);

    function handleClick(){
        console.log("button was clicked!")
    }

  return (
    <div>
      <p>Count: {count}</p>
      <button>Increment</button>
    </div>
  );
}
export default Counter;
```

Now you see if you click on the button, a message appears in the console log. This means that our handler is working.

Now let's update the function to increment the count, and attach it to the onClick handler, this way the user can interact with the component:

```
import React, { useState } from 'react';
```

26

```
function Counter() {
  const [count, setCount] = useState(0);

    function handleClick(){
        setCount(count + 1);
    }

  return (
    <div>
      <p>Count: {count}</p>
      <button onClick={handleClick}>Increment</button>
    </div>
  );
}
export default Counter;
```

Let's walk through the details of this working example:

1. **useState(0):** We use the useState hook to declare a state variable count, initializing it with 0, as well as providing a function setCount that will update the state.
2. **<p>Count: {count}</p>:** We use JSX to display the count value in the UI.
3. **<button onClick={handleClick}>Increment</button>:** We attach the handleClick function to the button's onClick event.

Now, when you click the button:

- The handleClick function is called.
- setCount(count + 1) is invoked, updating the count.
- React detects that the component's state has changed.
- React triggers a re-render of the component, updating the UI to reflect the new count value.

The button now increments the count on each click.

Practical Implementations: A Step-by-Step Approach

Let's enhance this example to be more practical. Imagine you are building a form that toggles the display of additional input fields when a checkbox is toggled. This time we'll introduce the onChange event.

First, let's build the base of the component:

```
import React, { useState } from 'react';

function ToggleFields() {
    const [showFields, setShowFields] = useState(false);

    return (
        <div>
            <label>
                Show additional fields:
                <input type="checkbox" />
            </label>
            {showFields &&
            <div style={{marginTop: '10px'}}>
                <label>
                    Email:
                    <input type="text" />
                </label>
            </div>
            }
        </div>
    )
}
export default ToggleFields;
```

The first thing you will notice is that, although we have added the showFields state using useState, our component doesn't react to our changes. Lets introduce an event listener, onChange, to the input element, as well as create a new function to handle the event.

```
import React, { useState } from 'react';

function ToggleFields() {
    const [showFields, setShowFields] = useState(false);

    function handleChange(event) {
        console.log(event.target.checked);
    }

    return (
        <div>
            <label>
                Show additional fields:
                <input type="checkbox" onChange={handleChange} />
            </label>
            {showFields &&
            <div style={{marginTop: '10px'}}>
                <label>
                    Email:
                    <input type="text" />
```

```
            </label>
        </div>
            }
        </div>
    )
}
export default ToggleFields;
```

Now, you can see in the console log that each time you click the check box, it logs true or false. Lets now use this information to set the showFields state by adding setShowFields in our function, with the updated code:

```
import React, { useState } from 'react';

function ToggleFields() {
    const [showFields, setShowFields] = useState(false);

    function handleChange(event) {
        setShowFields(event.target.checked);
    }

    return (
        <div>
            <label>
                Show additional fields:
                <input type="checkbox" onChange={handleChange} />
            </label>
            {showFields &&
            <div style={{marginTop: '10px'}}>
                <label>
                    Email:
                    <input type="text" />
                </label>
            </div>
            }
        </div>
    )
}
export default ToggleFields;
```

Here's a breakdown:

- **const [showFields, setShowFields] = useState(false);**: We create a state variable showFields to manage the visibility of the additional fields, and initialize it to false because we don't want to show the fields immediately.

- **<input type="checkbox" onChange={handleChange} />**: We attach the handleChange function to the checkbox's onChange event.
- **setShowFields(event.target.checked);**: Inside the event handler, we use the setShowFields function to update the showFields state based on whether the checkbox is checked or not.
- **{showFields && ...}**: Using conditional rendering, we only display the email input when showFields is true.

This example illustrates how state and events work together to create dynamic UI components. The form will now toggle the email field based on the users choice.

From my experience, I've found that clear naming conventions for both your state variables and event handlers are really crucial for maintainability and collaboration. Using names like count and handleClick might be fine for simple examples, but for bigger applications, this can become hard to decipher. This helps everyone on the team understand what is going on in the component at a glance.

Key Takeaways:

- State allows components to store and manage data that changes, it is crucial for making our react apps dynamic and responsive.
- Events enable components to respond to user interactions, and then using the handler functions, you can then update the component's state.
- useState is a hook that lets us manage state in functional components, as well as a function that updates the state and triggers UI updates.
- Careful consideration should be given to event handlers and state updates so that our React components remain performant and readable.

By understanding state and events, you now have the fundamental tools to create interactive and responsive user interfaces. These two concepts will be used going forward as we continue to explore react.

2.2 THE VIRTUAL DOM AND RECONCILIATION: UNDER THE HOOD

At its heart, React's performance stems from its innovative use of a **Virtual DOM** and an intelligent process called **Reconciliation**. These two concepts work in tandem to ensure that React applications remain fast and responsive, even when handling complex UI updates. Let's break it down step by step.

The Virtual DOM: A Lightweight Copy

Traditional web development typically involves directly manipulating the Real DOM using JavaScript. However, directly updating the Real DOM can be slow and resource-intensive. React addresses this by using a Virtual DOM.

Think of the Virtual DOM as a lightweight in-memory representation of the actual DOM. It's like a blueprint of your UI, constructed using JavaScript objects. When you update a component's state, React doesn't immediately modify the Real DOM. Instead, it creates a new version of the Virtual DOM to reflect those changes.

Why is this approach more efficient? Because manipulating JavaScript objects in memory is far faster than directly altering the browser's DOM. This means React can efficiently figure out what updates need to be made, before interacting with the real DOM.

Reconciliation: The Diffing Algorithm

Now that we have our old Virtual DOM and our new Virtual DOM, the question remains, how do we actually update the DOM efficiently? This is where **Reconciliation** comes into the picture. This process is where React compares the new Virtual DOM with the previous Virtual DOM, identifying the minimal number of changes necessary to update the actual DOM. This comparison is also called "diffing" because we are essentially looking for the difference between the two dom trees.

Reconciliation is at the heart of React's performance advantages. Instead of redrawing the entire UI, React intelligently figures out what has changed, which minimizes the impact to the performance of the browser. This process is also responsible for maintaining user experience so that React apps feel responsive.

A Step-by-Step View of the Process

Let's walk through a simplified version of what happens when a component's state changes:

1. **State Update:** A component's state is updated by calling its setter function (e.g. setCount from useState).
2. **Virtual DOM Creation:** React creates a new Virtual DOM, which is the updated version of the UI.

3. **Reconciliation (Diffing):** React compares the new Virtual DOM with the previous Virtual DOM. It identifies the minimal number of changes required to make the UI consistent with the new Virtual DOM.
4. **Real DOM Update:** React applies these minimal changes to the real DOM. This process is optimized for speed, as React only updates the parts of the actual DOM that have changed.

The reconciliation process is not a trivial task. React uses a heuristic algorithm to efficiently diff the two trees. This algorithm does not compare the two trees node by node, which is an O(n^3) operation, but instead uses a clever algorithm, with time complexity of O(n) to figure out how to update the real DOM.

Illustrative Example: A Dynamic List

To make this more concrete, let's consider a component that displays a dynamic list of items. As you may know, dynamically updating lists in the real DOM can be tricky because we are adding and removing elements.

Here's how React handles it efficiently:

```
import React, { useState } from 'react';

function DynamicList() {
    const [items, setItems] = useState([
        { id: 1, text: "Item 1" },
        { id: 2, text: "Item 2" },
        { id: 3, text: "Item 3" },
    ]);

    function addItem() {
        const newItem = {
            id: items.length + 1,
            text: `Item ${items.length + 1}`,
        };
        setItems([...items, newItem]);
    }

    function deleteItem(id) {
        setItems(items.filter((item) => item.id !== id));
    }
    return (
        <div>
            <ul>
                {items.map(item => (
                <li key={item.id}>
                    {item.text}
```

```
              <button onClick={() =>
deleteItem(item.id)}>Delete</button>
              </li>
         ))}
         </ul>
         <button onClick={addItem}>Add Item</button>
      </div>
   )
}
export default DynamicList;
```

In this example:

- The items state holds our list of objects.
- The addItem function adds a new item to the list, using setItems to set the updated array.
- The deleteItem function deletes an item from the list using filter and updates the state using setItems.
- The list is dynamically rendered with map.

Here's what happens when the state changes by calling the addItem or deleteItem functions:

1. **State change:** When we call setItems, react recognizes this as a change in state.
2. **New Virtual DOM:** React creates a new Virtual DOM, where the list items now reflect the new items or the removed items.
3. **Reconciliation:** React compares the new Virtual DOM with the previous Virtual DOM, identifies the minimal changes needed, such as added or removed <li> elements.
4. **Real DOM update:** React updates only the necessary parts of the real DOM, avoiding any unnecessary re-renders.

When adding an item, React just adds the new list item without re-rendering the entire list. When deleting an item, React just removes the deleted item.

Practical Implementations

While the Virtual DOM and reconciliation process is something that React takes care of automatically, there are some best practices that you can follow to maximize performance. Using the key prop in a list, is extremely important. If we didn't include the key prop in our <li> element, React would be forced to do a much more costly diffing process.

```
    {items.map(item => (
    <li key={item.id}>
        {item.text}
        <button onClick={() => deleteItem(item.id)}>Delete</button>
    </li>
))}
```

In this code, we use the key prop by passing in item.id. This allows React to uniquely identify each element in the array, improving rendering performance. This tells react which element in the array is which, and when it changes, React doesn't need to re-render the other list items.

Personal Insight

When I first started using React, I didn't pay much attention to the Virtual DOM and Reconciliation, I often treated React as a magical library that just worked. When I had to debug performance issues in a large application, I realized that ignoring the Virtual DOM will cause headaches. Understanding these core concepts will not only help improve performance, it will also give you a better insight into what is actually happening when you build React applications.

Key Takeaways:

- The Virtual DOM is a lightweight in-memory representation of the actual DOM, enabling efficient updates.
- Reconciliation is the process where React compares the new and old Virtual DOMs to identify minimal changes.
- React updates only the changed portions of the real DOM for improved performance and responsiveness.
- Using keys in lists helps React efficiently update the correct elements in a list.

By understanding the Virtual DOM and the reconciliation process, you will not only better understand how React works under the hood, but you will also be able to build better performing React applications. This concept will be essential when we discuss performance optimization going forward.

2.3 REACT HOOKS OVERVIEW: EMBRACING FUNCTIONALITY

React Hooks, introduced in React 16.8, are functions that let you "hook into" React state and lifecycle features from within functional components. Before Hooks, class components were the only way to manage state and lifecycle events. Hooks changed everything, allowing us to build complex React applications using only functional components.

Why React Hooks?

Hooks address several key challenges with class components:

- **Complexity of Class Components:** Class components often involve verbose syntax, making them harder to read, understand, and maintain.
- **Lifecycle Management:** Class components' lifecycle methods (like componentDidMount and componentDidUpdate) can be difficult to grasp and often lead to complex logic spread across multiple methods.
- **Code Reusability:** Reusing stateful logic across different class components is challenging and requires complex patterns like higher-order components or render props.

React Hooks provide solutions to these challenges by providing a simpler and more flexible way to manage state, side effects, and other React features directly within functional components.

Key Principles of Hooks

Before we get into examples, let's cover a few fundamental principles of React Hooks:

1. **Hooks are Functions:** Hooks are just JavaScript functions that let you "hook into" React features.
2. **Hooks are Used Inside Functional Components:** Hooks are only used inside of functional components and must be called at the top level of the component, not inside loops, conditional statements, or nested functions.
3. **Hooks Can Be Custom:** You can create your own custom hooks to extract and reuse stateful logic across multiple components.
4. **Hooks Don't Replace Class Components:** Hooks do not aim to replace class components, but provide a more elegant and concise approach for writing new React code.

Commonly Used React Hooks

Let's briefly introduce some of the most commonly used hooks. We will be expanding on each of these concepts in future sections.

- **useState:** This hook is used to add state to a functional component. We saw this in action in section 2.1, where we used it to increment a count when the button was clicked.
- **useEffect:** This hook allows you to perform side effects in a functional component, such as fetching data from an API, subscriptions, or directly modifying the DOM.
- **useContext:** This hook allows you to access the context, which is a tool to share data across the component tree, and is a fundamental concept in global state management.
- **useRef:** This hook allows you to create mutable references that persist across component renders, giving a component a way to persist data that is not a part of state, this could be used for DOM manipulation or to persist intervals or timeouts.
- **useReducer:** This hook provides an alternative to useState for managing more complex state logic.

Practical Implementation: A Step-by-Step Approach

Let's look at a practical example that combines multiple hooks into one component. We are going to build a simple form that uses useState and useEffect.

```
import React, { useState, useEffect } from 'react';

function SimpleForm() {
    const [name, setName] = useState('');
    const [email, setEmail] = useState('');
    const [submitted, setSubmitted] = useState(false);


    useEffect(() => {
        console.log("form rendered or state was updated.");
    }, [name, email])

    function handleSubmit(e) {
        e.preventDefault(); //prevent refresh
        setSubmitted(true);
    }
    return (
        <form onSubmit={handleSubmit}>
            <label>
                Name:
                <input type="text" value={name} onChange={e =>
setName(e.target.value)} />
```

```
          </label>
          <label>
              Email:
              <input type="email" value={email} onChange={e =>
setEmail(e.target.value)} />
          </label>
          <button type="submit">Submit</button>
          {submitted &&
          <div>
              <p>You have submitted {name} with email
{email}!</p>
          </div>
          }
      </form>
    )
}
export default SimpleForm;
```

Here is a breakdown:

- **useState for Form Inputs:** We use the useState hook to manage three state variables: name, email, and submitted, initializing them with empty strings, and false.
- **useEffect for Logging:** We use the useEffect hook to log a message to the console each time the component is rendered or the name or email state variables are updated. Notice we use the dependencies array [name, email] to only run the function only if those two state variables are updated.
- **Event Handlers:** For the inputs, we use onChange to update the corresponding state variables. In the form we use onSubmit which calls handleSubmit.
- **Form Submission:** When the submit button is clicked, handleSubmit is called, which sets the submitted state to true.
- **Conditional Rendering:** We conditionally render a message below the form when submitted is true.

This small example shows how multiple hooks work together to provide a way to build complex functionality.

Custom Hooks

The ability to create custom hooks is one of the best features of React hooks. It is a powerful way to share stateful logic across components, without relying on higher-order components or render props.

A custom hook is a function that starts with the word "use", and then calls other hooks within it.

Lets create a custom hook that implements a simple counter with an increment and decrement button.

```
import { useState } from "react";

function useCounter(initialValue = 0) {
    const [count, setCount] = useState(initialValue);

    function increment() {
        setCount(prevCount => prevCount + 1);
    }

    function decrement() {
        setCount(prevCount => prevCount - 1);
    }

    return {
      count,
      increment,
      decrement
    };
}

export default useCounter;
```

Now that we have our custom hook, we can use it in our component:

```
import React from "react";
import useCounter from "./useCounter";

function CustomCounter() {
    const { count, increment, decrement } = useCounter(100);

    return (
      <div>
          <p>Count: {count}</p>
          <button onClick={increment}>Increment</button>
          <button onClick={decrement}>Decrement</button>
      </div>
    );
}
export default CustomCounter;
```

Here's the breakdown:

- **useCounter**: Our custom hook, which manages the state for the counter.
- **Using our custom hook**: Inside of the component, we are using our custom hook and getting the count and our setter functions.
- **State Management**: When the buttons are clicked, we can see the counter incrementing.

We've successfully abstracted away the counter logic into its own hook and reused it in another component!

Personal Insights

When I first encountered React Hooks, I was a bit hesitant to embrace them. Class components and lifecycle methods were deeply ingrained in my React development process, but after a little time I realized hooks were just a better way to manage react. Not only was the code much simpler, but sharing code across the application was much easier. Now, I almost exclusively use functional components and hooks for new projects.

Key Takeaways:

- React Hooks are functions that allow us to use React state and lifecycle features within functional components.
- Hooks help us avoid the complexity of class components and provide a more straightforward way to manage state and side effects.
- Hooks are composable, meaning they can be combined to create complex and reusable logic.
- Hooks provide a way to extract and reuse stateful logic across components using custom hooks.

React Hooks have transformed the way we develop in React, making our code more readable, manageable, and reusable. As we continue, you'll see how we'll make use of hooks going forward.

2.4 USESTATE AND USEEFFECT IN ACTION: THE HEART OF REACT'S DYNAMISM

If you remember, React components were static without state. useState introduced in React 16.8, is what allows functional components to have their own state. useEffect on the other hand lets us manage side effects, like fetching data, or updating the DOM. These two concepts together allow functional components to now have the same features as class components, but with much less code.

useState: Adding State to Functional Components

At its core, useState is a hook that adds state to a functional component. It's like providing a component with memory, allowing it to store data that changes over time and triggers UI updates. Here's how it works:

1. **Declaration:** You declare a state variable by calling the useState hook inside your functional component:

```
import React, { useState } from 'react';

function MyComponent() {
  const [myState, setMyState] = useState(initialValue);
    //Rest of the component
}
```

- useState(initialValue): This function initializes the state variable with the initial value and returns an array of two values.
- myState: Represents the current value of our state, we can use this value to display on the screen.
- setMyState: Is a function that we use to update our state, and that will cause a re-render of the component.
- initialValue can be anything, for example a string, number, object, array, or even another function, this is the initial value of our state.

2. **Using the State:** You can access the current state value with myState in JSX and update it using setMyState. When setMyState is called with a new value, it causes the component to re-render.

Let's solidify our understanding with a simple example, a counter with an increment and decrement button:

```
import React, { useState } from 'react';

function Counter() {
    const [count, setCount] = useState(0);

    function increment() {
        setCount(count + 1);
    }
```

```
    function decrement() {
        setCount(count - 1);
    }
    return (
        <div>
            <p>Count: {count}</p>
            <button onClick={increment}>Increment</button>
            <button onClick={decrement}>Decrement</button>
        </div>
    )
}
export default Counter;
```

In this example:

- const [count, setCount] = useState(0); We are initializing our state with the useState function, passing in an initial value of 0. This returns the count and the setCount function, which we can use to update the count.
- We are using the count in our JSX element, and this value will be updated each time we call setCount.
- When the increment or decrement functions are called, setCount is called with either the incremented or decremented values.

useEffect: Managing Side Effects

useEffect is another essential hook that allows you to perform side effects in functional components. Side effects are anything outside the component logic, such as data fetching, setting timers, or updating the DOM directly.

1. **Declaration:** You declare the useEffect hook by calling it inside your functional component:

```
import React, { useEffect } from 'react';

function MyComponent() {
  useEffect(() => {
      // Code to perform side effects
      // This code is called after the component renders.

      return () => {
          // Optional cleanup code, which is called before each
subsequent effect or during unmounting.
      }
  }, [dependencies])
  //Rest of the component
```

}

- o useEffect(callback, [dependencies]): This function takes two arguments: a callback function to execute and an optional dependency array. The callback is executed after each render if the dependencies have changed.
- o The callback function is where we will write our logic, such as fetching data or manipulating the dom.
- o The optional cleanup function can be returned by the callback, which will be executed when the component unmounts.
- o The [dependencies] is an array of the dependencies of the side effect. It tells React to call the effect only if one of the values in the dependency array changes. If the array is empty ([]), it only runs on mount and unmount.

Let's look at an example that fetches data from an API and displays it on the screen using useEffect and useState. We will use the API https://jsonplaceholder.typicode.com/todos/1 which returns a json object.

```
import React, { useState, useEffect } from 'react';

function Todo() {
    const [todo, setTodo] = useState(null);
    const [loading, setLoading] = useState(true);

    useEffect(() => {
        fetch('https://jsonplaceholder.typicode.com/todos/1')
        .then(response => response.json())
        .then(data => {
            setTodo(data);
            setLoading(false);
        })
    }, [])

    if (loading) {
        return <p>Loading...</p>
    }
    if(!todo){
        return <p>Error!</p>
    }
    return (
        <div>
            <h1>{todo.title}</h1>
            <p>Completed: {todo.completed ? 'Yes' : 'No'}</p>
        </div>
    )
```

```
}
export default Todo;
```

Here's a step by step explanation:

- We initialize two state variables, todo, which stores the data from the API, and loading, which is true when the data is still loading.
- We use the useEffect hook. Notice, that we pass in an empty dependency array, [], which means that this function only runs on mount and unmount.
- In our useEffect function, we use fetch which makes a request to an API, then converts the response to json using .json().
- Then using the data from the API, we update the todo state using the setTodo function. We also update the loading state to false, to tell the component that we are done loading.
- Lastly, in the JSX we either display a loading message while loading, or display the todo object.

Practical Implementation: Combining useState and useEffect

Let's take a look at a practical implementation where we combine useState and useEffect. We are going to implement a simple search bar, that filters through our list of todos.

```
import React, { useState, useEffect } from 'react';
function SearchTodo() {
    const [todos, setTodos] = useState([]);
    const [searchTerm, setSearchTerm] = useState('');
    const [filteredTodos, setFilteredTodos] = useState([]);
    const [loading, setLoading] = useState(true);

    useEffect(() => {
        fetch('https://jsonplaceholder.typicode.com/todos')
            .then(response => response.json())
            .then(data => {
                setTodos(data);
                setLoading(false)
                setFilteredTodos(data);
            })
    }, [])

    useEffect(() => {
        const results = todos.filter(todo =>
```

```
todo.title.toLowerCase().includes(searchTerm.toLowerCase())
        );
      setFilteredTodos(results);
    }, [searchTerm, todos]);


    function handleChange(event) {
        setSearchTerm(event.target.value);
    }
        if (loading) {
            return <p>Loading...</p>
        }
    return (
        <div>
            <input
                type="text"
                placeholder="Search for todos..."
                value={searchTerm}
                onChange={handleChange}
            />
            <ul>
                {filteredTodos.map(todo => (
                    <li key={todo.id}>{todo.title}</li>
                ))}
            </ul>
        </div>
    )
}
export default SearchTodo;
```

Here's what's happening:

- We are initializing 4 state variables, todos, which contains all of the todos, searchTerm, which is the value of the search bar, filteredTodos, which is the list of the filtered todos, and loading, which is true when we have not finished fetching the data.
- The first useEffect hook, fetches the todo list from the API. We can see that the dependency array is an empty array, which means that this function runs only on mount.
- The second useEffect hook, filters through the todos list to display filtered todos.
- We create a function handleChange, which updates the search bar's value.
- Lastly, we display a loading message when the data is still loading, a search bar, and a list of todos based on the filteredTodos state.

In this example, you can type into the search bar and see that the list of todos are updated based on the search.

Personal Insights

As someone who has worked with React for a while, I've come to appreciate how elegantly useState and useEffect handle state and side effects. While class components offered similar functionality, Hooks make the logic cleaner and easier to follow, leading to code that is more maintainable. I also use custom hooks to reuse logic in different parts of the application, which further reduces redundancy in my code.

Key Takeaways:

- useState lets functional components manage local state, which is the core of interactivity in React.
- useEffect manages side effects, allowing components to interact with the external world and update the DOM.
- useEffect accepts a dependencies array, which specifies when to call the side effect based on changes in state or props.

By understanding useState and useEffect you have gained two very powerful tools that will allow you to build the most complicated applications. These are the essential concepts that we will be using as we continue to explore advanced topics.

CHAPTER 3: ADVANCED COMPONENT PATTERNS

In this chapter, we move beyond the basics of components, state, and hooks. We're going to explore advanced patterns that help tackle common challenges in React development, such as state management, code reuse, and performance optimization. These patterns are the secret sauce of seasoned React developers, and understanding them will greatly enhance your ability to craft robust applications.

3.1 CONTEXT API FOR STATE MANAGEMENT

We've seen how useState can be used for managing local component state, but when it comes to sharing data between multiple components, especially across different parts of your component tree, using props alone can become cumbersome and difficult to manage. This is where React's **Context API** comes into play.

The Context API provides a way to share state that can be accessed by any component in a specific part of your application, eliminating the need to "prop drill" data down through multiple layers of components. It allows components to *subscribe* to the changes of the shared state.

Let's go over the key steps involved with context:

1. **Creating a Context:** We will first create a context object using the function createContext():

```
import { createContext } from 'react';

const MyContext = createContext(defaultValue);
```

   - createContext(defaultValue): This function returns a context object, with an optional default value.
   - MyContext: The returned value of the createContext() function, which is a react context object.
2. **Wrapping the component tree:** Next, we wrap our desired component tree using the Provider component. The Provider allows our component tree to access the shared data through a property called value:

```
    import React from "react";
import MyContext from "./MyContext";
function ProviderComponent({ children, value }){
    return <MyContext.Provider value={value}>
       {children}
      </MyContext.Provider>
}
export default ProviderComponent;
```

- o <MyContext.Provider>: This component takes our created
  MyContext and passes in our value through its value prop.
- o children: Any components that are rendered as the children of this
  Provider will be able to access our context.
- o value: This is our shared state, any updates in value will cause all
  components using the context to rerender.
3. **Consuming the Context:** Finally, components within the subtree can use the
context using the useContext hook:

```
    import React, { useContext } from "react";
import MyContext from "./MyContext";
function ConsumerComponent() {
  const contextValue = useContext(MyContext);
  //Rest of the component
}
```

- o useContext(MyContext): This function returns the value prop from
  the closest provider higher up the component tree.

Practical Example: Theme Switching

Let's take a look at a practical example of using the Context API to allow our
application to switch between themes.

First, we must create our context object: ThemeContext.js

```
    import { createContext } from 'react';
const ThemeContext = createContext({
  theme: 'light',
  toggleTheme: () => {}
});
export default ThemeContext;
```

Next, we create our ThemeProvider component, ThemeProvider.js, that wraps our components and allows us to update our shared state.

```
import React, { useState } from "react";
import ThemeContext from "./ThemeContext";
function ThemeProvider({ children }){
  const [theme, setTheme] = useState('light');
  function toggleTheme(){
    setTheme(prevTheme => prevTheme === 'light' ? 'dark' :
'light');
  }
  return (
      <ThemeContext.Provider value={{theme, toggleTheme}}>
        {children}
      </ThemeContext.Provider>
  )
}
export default ThemeProvider;
```

Lastly, here is our ThemeSwitcher component, which uses the context using the useContext hook. ThemeSwitcher.js

```
import React, { useContext } from "react";
import ThemeContext from "./ThemeContext";

function ThemeSwitcher(){
  const {theme, toggleTheme } = useContext(ThemeContext);
  return (
      <div style={{
        padding: '10px',
        backgroundColor: theme === 'light' ? 'white' : 'black',
        color: theme === 'light' ? 'black' : 'white'
      }}>
        <p>The theme is {theme}</p>
        <button onClick={toggleTheme}>Toggle Theme</button>
      </div>
  )
}
export default ThemeSwitcher;
```

Here, we are using the theme from the ThemeContext, and the styles are dynamically updated based on the value of the theme in the context.

Lastly, lets use the components that we have made:

```
import React from 'react';
```

```
import ThemeProvider from "./ThemeProvider";
import ThemeSwitcher from "./ThemeSwitcher";

function App() {
  return (
    <ThemeProvider>
      <ThemeSwitcher />
    </ThemeProvider>
  );
}

export default App;
```

In this implementation:

- We created a ThemeContext, that is shared by our components.
- We created a ThemeProvider, that provides our component tree with access to the context, and also provides the theme state, and toggleTheme function.
- Finally, our ThemeSwitcher consumes the context, and updates the style of the component based on the current value in context.

This example demonstrates how we are passing the context, without passing data down through multiple props.

Personal Insight: When I first started using React, I didn't appreciate the power of context. I would often pass data down through multiple layers, which became difficult to manage. When I was working on a large application I found it challenging to trace my data. Once I understood the Context API, it completely changed my approach. I try to use it now for things that are shared throughout the application such as theming, or authentication.

3.2 HIGHER-ORDER COMPONENTS (HOCS): ENHANCING COMPONENTS THROUGH COMPOSITION

In React, Higher-Order Components (HOCs) are an advanced technique that allows you to reuse component logic. A Higher-Order Component is not a component itself, but instead is a function that takes in a component as an argument, and returns a new enhanced component. HOCs help to avoid duplication of code, by abstracting functionality into a reusable function.

Understanding the HOC Pattern

The basic structure of a HOC looks like this:

```
function withEnhancedFunctionality(WrappedComponent) {
  return function EnhancedComponent(props) {
    // Add additional logic or modify props here
    return <WrappedComponent {...props} />;
  };
}
```

Let's break down the pieces of this pattern:

- withEnhancedFunctionality: This is our higher-order component function, that takes in the component that we will be enhancing.
- WrappedComponent: This is the original component that we are enhancing.
- EnhancedComponent: This is the new component that we return from the HOC. Here we can add any additional functionality that we want, and return the WrappedComponent with all of the original props, and optionally some additional props if we want to.

How HOCs Enhance Components

HOCs enhance components by:

- **Adding Logic:** HOCs can add additional functionality or logic to the wrapped component, such as managing state, handling authentication, or logging actions.
- **Modifying Props:** HOCs can modify or add new props to the wrapped component, enabling components to receive additional context.
- **Reusability:** The logic added by HOCs can be easily reused across multiple components, preventing code duplication.
- **Non-Intrusive:** HOCs do not modify the original component, thus preventing errors in the core functionality of the component.

Practical Implementation: Logging Functionality

Let's explore a practical implementation of a HOC that adds logging functionality to a component. We'll create a withLogging HOC that logs when a component is mounted and when it is unmounted.

Here's our withLogging HOC:

```
    import React, { useEffect } from 'react';
function withLogging(WrappedComponent){
    return function EnhancedComponent(props) {
        useEffect(() => {
            console.log(`Component ${WrappedComponent.name}
mounted.`);

            return () => {
                console.log(`Component ${WrappedComponent.name}
unmounted.`);
            }
        }, [])
        return <WrappedComponent {...props} />
    }
}
export default withLogging;
```

Here is what we are doing:

- Our withLogging takes in the component that we want to log, and then returns an enhanced component.
- We are using useEffect with an empty dependency array to log when a component mounts, and we are also using the cleanup function to log when a component unmounts.
- Lastly we are returning the WrappedComponent with all the original props.

Now, let's create a simple component that we will wrap with our withLogging HOC, MyComponent.js:

```
    import React from 'react';
function MyComponent({message}){
    return (
        <p>
            {message}
        </p>
    )
}
export default MyComponent;
```

Now lets use our HOC in another component, EnhancedComponent.js:

```
    import React from 'react';
import withLogging from "./withLogging";
import MyComponent from './MyComponent';

function EnhancedComponent(){
```

```
    return <MyComponent message="This is a test message"/>
}

export default withLogging(EnhancedComponent);
```

Here's what's going on:

- We are importing our withLogging HOC that we have made, as well as our original component MyComponent.
- Then we are using the HOC to wrap the EnhancedComponent. This is the magic of higher order components!

Now, when you render EnhancedComponent in your application, you'll see the log messages in the console.

Practical Implementation: Authentication

Another common use case for HOCs is to manage authentication. Let's expand on what we have done previously by implementing a HOC that will protect our components from unauthenticated users, withAuthentication.js:

```
    import React from 'react';
function withAuthentication(WrappedComponent){
    return function EnhancedComponent(props){
        const isLoggedIn = true; // Replace this with an actual
auth check
        if(!isLoggedIn){
          return (
            <div>
              <p>You are not logged in!</p>
            </div>
          )
        }
        return <WrappedComponent {...props} />
    }
}
export default withAuthentication;
```

Here is the ProtectedComponent that is enhanced with the authentication functionality, ProtectedComponent.js:

```
    import React from 'react';
import withAuthentication from "./withAuthentication";
```

```
function ProtectedComponent(){
  return (
      <p>This component is protected</p>
  )
}
export default withAuthentication(ProtectedComponent);
```

- withAuthentication checks the isLoggedIn variable (replace with your actual authentication check), and if it is false then we display a log in message, otherwise the wrapped component is displayed.
- The ProtectedComponent is our original component that is being enhanced.

Personal Insights

HOCs were a really common pattern when I first started developing React. They are really useful when you need to add reusable functionality to multiple components in a way that doesn't break the functionality of the component. HOCs are also a very good way of learning about how react works under the hood, and how components are actually just functions that return jsx.

Key Takeaways:

- Higher-Order Components (HOCs) are functions that enhance components without modifying their original functionality.
- HOCs take a component as an argument and return a new enhanced component.
- They help abstract common logic and make components more reusable.
- While HOCs were common before, with hooks you can implement similar behavior using custom hooks.

By understanding HOCs, you'll be able to appreciate a common pattern in the React community. Although the pattern is less common today, understanding it will help you appreciate many different patterns that React provides.

3.3 RENDER PROPS AND COMPOSITION: FLEXIBLE COMPONENT DESIGN

Render Props and Composition are two patterns that offer alternatives to Higher-Order Components (HOCs) for reusing and sharing functionality in React. They both leverage the way React components work to create reusable logic.

Render Props: Dynamic Content through Function Props

A **render prop** is a function prop that a component uses to render dynamic content. Instead of the component directly rendering a specific element, it calls the render prop function and lets *that* function decide what should be rendered.

Let's look at the structure of a render prop component:

```
import React from 'react';

function MyComponent({ render }) {
  // Perform some actions and generate data
  const data = { value: "Data from component" };

  //Call the render prop to render something
  return <div>{render(data)}</div>;
}

export default MyComponent;
```

Here's a breakdown:

- MyComponent is the component using a render prop.
- render is the render prop function, which will be used to determine what to render.
- Inside of MyComponent, we are performing some actions, and then we are using the render prop function with the data as an argument.

A component that uses this render prop looks like this:

```
import React from 'react';
import MyComponent from "./MyComponent";

function MyConsumerComponent(){
    return (
        <MyComponent render={
            (data) => {
                return <p> {data.value} </p>
            }
        }/>
    )
```

```
}
export default MyConsumerComponent;
```

Here's what's happening:

- MyConsumerComponent: This component is using the MyComponent and is passing in a render prop function, using the render property.
- The function that is passed into MyComponent as the render prop will be called using the data.

In essence, render props let you pass a function to a component that has control of *how* to render itself. This allows you to create extremely customizable and reusable components.

Practical Implementation: Mouse Tracking

Let's create a practical example of a Mouse Tracker using render props. This is a component that tracks mouse coordinates, and then allows a child component to have access to that data.

Here's our Mouse Tracker component using render props, MouseTracker.js:

```
import React, { useState, useEffect } from 'react';

function MouseTracker({ render }){
  const [mouse, setMouse] = useState({ x: 0, y: 0 });
  useEffect(() => {
    function handleMouseMove(e){
      setMouse({
          x: e.clientX,
          y: e.clientY,
      });
    }
    window.addEventListener('mousemove', handleMouseMove);

    return () => {
      window.removeEventListener('mousemove', handleMouseMove);
    }
  }, []);

  return <div>{render(mouse)}</div>
}
export default MouseTracker;
```

Let's walk through the code:

- MouseTracker takes in a function as a render prop called render.
- The component then keeps track of the mouse coordinates and stores it using the mouse state.
- We are using useEffect to add and remove event listeners, to listen to the movement of the mouse.
- Finally the render prop function is called, and the mouse coordinates are passed into it as an argument.

Here is a component that renders the Mouse coordinates on the screen using the MouseTracker: MyComponent.js

```
import React from 'react';
import MouseTracker from "./MouseTracker";

function MyComponent() {
    return (
        <MouseTracker
            render={(mouse) => (
                <p>
                    Mouse coordinates: x: {mouse.x}, y: {mouse.y}
                </p>
            )}
        />
    );
}
export default MyComponent;
```

Here is a breakdown of our code:

- MyComponent: Is the component that consumes the MouseTracker.
- We are passing in a render prop function to the MouseTracker that renders the coordinates on the screen.
- The mouse coordinates are dynamically updated when the mouse moves.

Using a render prop function, we are able to reuse our logic to track the position of the mouse.

Composition: Building Components with Children

Composition in React is a pattern that encourages creating complex components by combining simpler ones. It relies on the principle of breaking down UI elements into smaller, reusable pieces. The most common example of composition is using the children prop, where any components you pass into a component is passed through this children prop.

Let's look at a basic example of a Layout Component:

```
import React from 'react';

function Layout({ children }) {
    return (
        <div className="layout">
            <header>
                <h1>Header</h1>
            </header>
            <main>{children}</main>
            <footer>
                <p>Footer</p>
            </footer>
        </div>
    );
}

export default Layout;
```

Here's what's happening:

- Layout takes a children prop, which will be passed in by components that use the Layout component.
- The Layout will display a basic layout structure using a header, main, and a footer.

A component that uses the Layout component:

```
import React from 'react';
import Layout from "./Layout";
function Page(){
    return (
        <Layout>
            <p>This is the page content</p>
        </Layout>
    )
}
export default Page;
```

- Here the Page component is using the Layout component, and it is passing the paragraph into the Layout using the children prop.

Composition is the core idea behind react, using small composable building blocks to construct the UI, instead of building monolithic components.

Practical Implementation: Alert Component

Let's create a reusable Alert component using composition. The alert component will take in a component in its children, and will wrap it in a div, and add a header to it.

Alert.js:

```
import React from 'react';

function Alert({children, message}){
    return (
        <div className="alert">
            <h3>{message}</h3>
            {children}
        </div>
    );
}
export default Alert;
```

- Alert takes in a message prop that is displayed as the header. It also takes in children that are displayed in the alert box.

And here is a component that uses the Alert component: MyComponent.js:

```
import React from 'react';
import Alert from "./Alert";

function MyComponent(){
    return (
      <Alert message="This is a warning">
         <p>This is the alert message.</p>
      </Alert>
    );
}
export default MyComponent;
```

- MyComponent uses the Alert component and passes a message and some text.

With composition, you're combining small, focused components to build larger, more complex ones, creating a very flexible system.

Personal Insight

When I first learned React, I would always create huge, monolithic components that did everything, and it was difficult to reuse my code. It was also very difficult to maintain the code and debug it. When I started to use the Render Prop and Composition patterns, I found that my code was more organized, easier to reuse, and more maintainable.

Key Takeaways:

- Render Props let you pass a function to a component, allowing dynamic rendering, this gives the consumers of your components ultimate control of how to render.
- Composition encourages creating complex components by combining simpler ones using techniques like the children prop.
- These patterns allow for highly customizable and reusable components.

Understanding Render Props and Composition helps you approach React development in a more flexible and dynamic way. These patterns are excellent for creating flexible and reusable UI libraries.

3.4 PERFORMANCE OPTIMIZATION WITH MEMOIZATION: CACHING FOR SPEED

Memoization is a performance optimization technique where we cache the results of expensive function calls and reuse them if the inputs haven't changed. Think of it as a way to avoid doing the same work repeatedly. In React, memoization helps to reduce unnecessary component re-renders, resulting in a smoother and faster user experience.

React provides two hooks for memoization: useMemo and useCallback. These hooks allow us to memoize both values and functions, giving us fine-grained control over when a component or function re-evaluates.

useMemo: Caching Values

The useMemo hook memoizes the result of an expensive calculation or value. It will only recalculate the value when one of the provided dependencies changes.

Here's the basic structure of useMemo:

```
import React, { useMemo } from 'react';

function MyComponent({ data }) {
    const memoizedValue = useMemo(() => {
        // Perform expensive calculation here
        return calculatedValue;
    }, [dependencies]);

    //Use the memoized value
}
```

Let's walk through the details:

- useMemo(() => { ... }, [dependencies]): The useMemo hook takes in two arguments:
    - A function that contains the expensive calculation that you want to memoize.
    - An array of dependencies. React will only re-execute this function if one of the dependencies changes.
- memoizedValue: Represents the cached value returned from the callback function.

Practical Implementation: Expensive Calculation

Let's look at a practical example using useMemo that demonstrates how we can use it to reduce unnessary re-renders.

```
import React, { useState, useMemo } from 'react';

function MyComponent({ data }) {
    const [count, setCount] = useState(0);

    const expensiveCalculation = useMemo(() => {
        console.log("performing expensive calculation")
        let sum = 0;
        for (let i = 0; i < 100000000; i++) {
            sum += data + i;
```

```
        }
        return sum;
    }, [data]);

    function handleClick(){
        setCount(prevCount => prevCount + 1);
    }

    return (
        <div>
            <p>Count: {count}</p>
            <button onClick={handleClick}>Increment</button>
            <p>Expensive Calculation: {expensiveCalculation}</p>
        </div>
    );
}
export default MyComponent;
```

Here's what's happening:

- We have an expensive calculation, which is calculated using useMemo.
- The expensive calculation is only performed if the data prop changes.
- If we call handleClick, it will update the count variable. However, the expensiveCalculation will not rerun, as the dependency has not changed, resulting in improved performance.

useCallback: Caching Functions

The useCallback hook memoizes functions, not values. It prevents function re-creation on each render, which is essential when passing functions as props to child components.

Here's the structure of useCallback:

```
    import React, { useCallback } from 'react';

function MyComponent({ callbackFunction }) {
    const memoizedCallback = useCallback(() => {
      // Perform actions here
    }, [dependencies]);
}
```

Let's break down this structure:

- useCallback(() => { ... }, [dependencies]): The useCallback takes in two arguments:
    - A callback function that you want to memoize.
    - An array of dependencies that are used in the callback. React will only re-create this callback if one of the dependencies changes.
- memoizedCallback: This is a function that is cached and will remain the same unless its dependencies have changed.

Practical Implementation: Preventing Child Component Re-renders

Let's expand on our previous example by using useCallback. We are going to create a Child component, and pass a memoized callback from a parent component, ParentComponent.js:

```
import React, { useState, useCallback } from 'react';
import ChildComponent from "./ChildComponent";

function ParentComponent(){
    const [count, setCount] = useState(0);
    const incrementCount = useCallback(() => {
        setCount(prevCount => prevCount + 1);
    }, []);

    return (
        <div>
            <p>Count: {count}</p>
            <ChildComponent onClick={incrementCount} />
        </div>
    );
}
export default ParentComponent;
```

ChildComponent.js:

```
import React from 'react';
function ChildComponent({ onClick }){
    console.log("Child Component re-rendered!");
    return <button onClick={onClick}>Increment</button>
}
export default ChildComponent;
```

Here is a breakdown of what is happening:

- The ParentComponent uses useCallback to memoize the incrementCount function, so that it does not get re-created on each render.
- The ChildComponent then uses the onClick prop, which is our function.
- If we didn't use useCallback, each time that the parent component re-renders, then it would create a new function and pass it to the child component, causing it to re-render, even though nothing changed. By using useCallback, the function only gets created once, and will be the same function going forward.

Key Considerations When Using Memoization

While memoization is powerful, it's essential to use it wisely:

- **Do Not Overuse:** Memoization comes with its own overhead. If the calculation isn't truly expensive, the overhead of memoizing could outweigh its benefits.
- **Only Use With Expensive Operations:** Use memoization with expensive operations that cause performance issues, such as complex calculations.
- **Dependencies are Key:** Carefully specify dependencies for both useMemo and useCallback, as improper dependency arrays will either cause unnecessary recomputations or cause errors because stale data will be used.

Personal Insight

When I first learned about memoization, I thought I had to use it everywhere. However, after working on several applications I realized that it can sometimes hurt performance, as there is overhead with using these functions. You should only use memoization with operations or functions that are costly, and when you need to prevent unnecessary re-renders of a component. When your application starts slowing down, it's important to use the React profiler to measure your performance. This way you can determine what is truly causing the performance problems, instead of guessing.

Key Takeaways:

- Memoization is a performance optimization technique that involves caching results of expensive operations and reusing them if inputs don't change.
- useMemo memoizes values, avoiding expensive calculations on every render.
- useCallback memoizes functions, preventing function re-creation on every render.

- Memoization can significantly improve the performance of your React applications, as long as it is used correctly.

By mastering memoization with useMemo and useCallback, you'll be able to fine-tune your React applications for optimal performance. This will help you to provide the best possible user experience.

CHAPTER 4: EFFICIENT STATE MANAGEMENT

Managing state effectively is critical for creating robust and scalable React applications. As our applications grow in complexity, it becomes more crucial to choose the right approach for managing state. This chapter will guide you through the landscape of state management, providing practical insights and best practices.

4.1 WHEN TO USE LOCAL VS. GLOBAL STATE: CHOOSING THE RIGHT TOOL

Deciding where to store your application's state is an important decision you will be making throughout the development process. There are two main places that you can store state: local component state or global application state. Both are very important, and using them appropriately is crucial.

Local Component State: Keeping Things Close

Local state is managed within a single component, typically using the useState hook. It's like a component's personal memory, specific to its rendering and lifecycle. Using local state is very good when the state is not shared between components.

Local state is appropriate when:

- **The data is specific to one component:** When a piece of state is only relevant to a single component, storing it locally will keep our component focused on its purpose, and will also be easier to maintain and debug. An example of this could be the form values in an input field, or a modal's visibility. These are usually isolated to a single component.
- **The state doesn't need to be shared:** Local state is the right approach when the state isn't needed by other components in the application. This makes the component self-contained and easier to reason about.
- **Simple State Management:** For simple UI elements that don't have complex logic or dependencies, local state is usually good enough. For example a button that toggles visibility, or a counter.

Practical Implementation: A Simple Toggle

Let's illustrate a practical example where we use local state with a simple toggle component that opens and closes:

```
import React, { useState } from 'react';

function Toggle() {
  const [isOpen, setIsOpen] = useState(false);
  function handleToggle() {
    setIsOpen(!isOpen);
  }
  return (
    <div>
      <button onClick={handleToggle}>{isOpen ? 'Close' :
'Open'}</button>
      {isOpen && <p>This content is now visible</p>}
    </div>
  );
}
export default Toggle;
```

Here's a step-by-step breakdown:

1. **State initialization:** const [isOpen, setIsOpen] = useState(false); initializes the state variable isOpen to false using useState.
2. **Toggle Functionality:** The handleToggle function is called on button click, and it updates the isOpen state by toggling its value.
3. **Conditional Rendering:** The paragraph is displayed based on the isOpen state, using conditional rendering.

This is an ideal situation for local state, because this component's state is only used inside of this component, and is not required by any other component in the application.

Global Application State: Sharing Across the Application

Global state, on the other hand, is state that is shared across multiple components throughout the application, instead of just a single component. This data needs to be accessed by other components, and can be updated by other components.

Global state is appropriate when:

- **State is shared across multiple components:** When you have data that needs to be accessed and modified by different parts of your application.

Examples of this are a user's authentication status, or the cart items in an ecommerce application.

- **Data needs to be passed across distant components:** When data is needed by components that are far apart in the component tree. This would mean that you have to pass down data using multiple props, and global state is a better solution for this.
- **State Logic is Complex:** When you need complex state updates that need to occur as a result of a number of different actions throughout the application, global state is the way to go.
- **Preserving State Across Routes:** In single-page applications, you may need to preserve state when navigating between different routes. This is a good use case for global state.

Practical Implementation: User Authentication

Let's take a look at an example of where global state would be used. The best example for this would be a user authentication system, where multiple components need to know the current state of the user, and also be able to modify the state of the user.

```javascript
import React, { useState, createContext, useContext } from 'react';

//Create the context
const AuthContext = createContext({
    isLoggedIn: false,
    login: () => { },
    logout: () => { },
});

function AuthProvider({ children }) {
    const [isLoggedIn, setIsLoggedIn] = useState(false);
    function login() {
        setIsLoggedIn(true);
    }
    function logout() {
        setIsLoggedIn(false);
    }

    const value = {
        isLoggedIn,
        login,
        logout,
    };

    return <AuthContext.Provider value={value}>{children}</AuthContext.Provider>;
```

```
}

//Create a custom hook for accessing the state
function useAuth() {
    return useContext(AuthContext);
}

// Components that will use the state:
function LoginButton() {
    const { isLoggedIn, login, logout } = useAuth();
    function handleClick() {
        if (isLoggedIn) {
            logout();
        } else {
            login();
        }
    }
    return <button onClick={handleClick}>{isLoggedIn ? 'Log Out' :
'Log In'}</button>;
}

function Dashboard() {
    const { isLoggedIn } = useAuth();
    return (
        <div>
            {isLoggedIn && <p>You are logged in</p>}
            {!isLoggedIn && <p>You are logged out</p>}
        </div>
    );
}

// Main component
function App() {
    return (
        <AuthProvider>
            <LoginButton />
            <Dashboard />
        </AuthProvider>
    );
}
export default App;
```

Here's a detailed explanation:

1. **AuthContext Creation**: We are creating the AuthContext using the createContext function, to store our state and its setter functions.

2. **AuthProvider**: Our provider will keep track of the isLoggedIn state and the login and logout functions, as well as allow our child components access to these.
3. **useAuth Hook**: The useAuth hook returns our provider, so that we can use this hook in any of our components to consume the AuthContext.
4. **LoginButton**: We are using our useAuth hook to display the "Log In" or "Log Out" button, and to also trigger a change in the state.
5. **Dashboard**: We are also using our useAuth hook to display information about the login status.
6. **App**: Finally in our App component, we are wrapping our LoginButton and Dashboard component with the AuthProvider, so that our components are able to use the AuthContext.

Here's why this is a good use case for global state:

- **Shared Across Components:** Multiple components, such as the LoginButton and the Dashboard, all need access to this state.
- **Data modification in multiple components:** Both the LoginButton and the Dashboard are able to modify the state, when the user clicks the "Log In" or "Log Out" button.
- **Complex Logic:** The component needs to track the user's authentication status, which should not be coupled into a single component.

Personal Insight

When I first started developing with React, I tried to put most of my state into the component local state, which caused many headaches when trying to access data from different components. I often found myself passing props down multiple levels, when the data should have been stored in global state. Once I started using global state management, and being intentional about how I use local state, I found that my application became much easier to maintain, and debug.

Key Takeaways:

- Local state is best used for data that is only relevant to a single component. This helps to keep components self-contained, and simple to understand.
- Global state should be used for data that is used by many different components and requires complex logic to modify the state.
- Carefully consider where to store your application state. Starting with local state can help you avoid over-engineering. Then move to global state when your app needs it.

By understanding the trade-offs between local and global state, you'll be able to create React applications that are not only more performant but also more maintainable and easier to scale as they grow. Making intentional decisions about which state to store where is extremely important.

4.2 USING CONTEXT API AND CUSTOM HOOKS: A POWERFUL COMBINATION

In the previous chapter, we explored the Context API for sharing state across components, and we also touched on the topic of using custom hooks to reuse logic. Now, let's look at combining the power of the Context API and Custom Hooks to provide a more elegant way to manage your application's state. The Context API and custom hooks are very powerful, and together they can greatly improve your state management capabilities.

Context API for Sharing State

As we know, the Context API is a built-in React feature that enables you to share state between components without having to pass props down multiple levels. It works with a Provider component, which provides the state, and a consumer, that can subscribe to the changes. This is an extremely powerful way to manage state.

Custom Hooks for Reusable Logic

We can also use custom hooks to extract and share component logic. These custom hooks can then use other hooks inside of them such as useState, useEffect, and the Context API. This allows you to reuse logic across components, making them much more maintainable.

By combining the Context API and custom hooks, we create a very powerful way of managing and sharing our application state, while being able to reuse code and logic across many components.

Practical Implementation: Theme Management

Let's create a practical example, where we are going to be using a custom hook, along with the Context API to manage the state of our application's theme.

First, we will create our context that will share the theme values, as well as a function that we will use to change the theme.

ThemeContext.js:

```
import React, { createContext } from 'react';
const ThemeContext = createContext({
    theme: 'light',
    toggleTheme: () => { },
});
export default ThemeContext;
```

Next, we create the ThemeProvider, which is the provider of our theme. This is also where we store the state of our theme, as well as the toggleTheme function. ThemeProvider.js:

```
import React, { useState } from 'react';
import ThemeContext from './ThemeContext';
function ThemeProvider({ children }) {
    const [theme, setTheme] = useState('light');

    function toggleTheme() {
        setTheme(prevTheme => prevTheme === 'light' ? 'dark' :
'light');
    }

    const value = {
        theme,
        toggleTheme,
    };

    return (
        <ThemeContext.Provider value={value}>
            {children}
        </ThemeContext.Provider>
    );
}
export default ThemeProvider;
```

Here's a breakdown of this component:

- We initialize the theme as light using the useState hook.
- We create a function to toggle the theme using the setTheme function.
- Lastly we are using the ThemeContext.Provider to provide the state to all the child components, which also includes our theme toggler.

Now we will create our custom hook, useTheme.js. This allows us to easily access the theme and the theme toggle across different components.

```
import React, { useContext } from 'react';
import ThemeContext from './ThemeContext';
function useTheme() {
    return useContext(ThemeContext);
}
export default useTheme;
```

Now, let's see how we can use this in components: ThemeButton.js

```
import React from 'react';
import useTheme from './useTheme';
function ThemeButton() {
    const { theme, toggleTheme } = useTheme();
    return (
        <button
            onClick={toggleTheme}
        >
            Toggle to {theme === 'light' ? 'dark' : 'light'} theme
        </button>
    );
}
export default ThemeButton;
```

ThemedComponent.js:

```
import React from 'react';
import useTheme from './useTheme';
function ThemedComponent({ children }) {
    const { theme } = useTheme();
    return (
        <div style={{
            padding: '10px',
            backgroundColor: theme === 'light' ? 'white' : 'black',
            color: theme === 'light' ? 'black' : 'white',
        }}>
            {children}
        </div>
    );
}
export default ThemedComponent;
```

And finally, here is our main component where we use it, App.js:

```
    import React from 'react';
import ThemeProvider from "./ThemeProvider";
import ThemedComponent from "./ThemedComponent";
import ThemeButton from "./ThemeButton";
function App(){
    return (
        <ThemeProvider>
            <ThemedComponent>
                <p>This component is themed</p>
                <ThemeButton />
            </ThemedComponent>
        </ThemeProvider>
    );
}
export default App;
```

Here's what's happening in this example:

- We are wrapping the components with the ThemeProvider component. All components that are nested in here will be able to use the shared state.
- We create a ThemeContext using createContext, this object is used for consuming and providing the theme.
- We then create our ThemeProvider component, where we set our theme state, and the toggleTheme function, and then pass it as the provider's value prop, which is what is provided to all child components.
- The useTheme custom hook simplifies the access to the context, and provides the consumer with easy access to the state and its setter function.
- The ThemeButton uses our useTheme hook to get the theme, and toggleTheme function from our context.
- The ThemedComponent uses the context, and styles the component dynamically based on the current value of the theme.

With this combination, you've created a more scalable and organized way to manage your application's theme. Any component can now access the theme using the useTheme custom hook, and can also update the theme through the same hook.

Benefits of This Approach

- **Centralized State:** The Context API allows for a centralized management of shared states.
- **Clean Access**: The use of custom hooks simplifies the way we access state and functionality.
- **Code Reusability:** Custom hooks make it easy to share state logic across multiple components.

- **Improved Structure:** This combination improves the structure of our application, making components more focused on their individual responsibilities.

Personal Insight

I've found that combining the Context API with custom hooks leads to a much more pleasant and organized development experience. It strikes a good balance between ease of use, and having a maintainable structure. Whenever I have application-wide state, this is always my first choice. I also appreciate the ability to make more composable code, and that I can extract all the stateful logic into a custom hook.

Key Takeaways:

- Combining the Context API with custom hooks is a great way to create powerful and scalable state management systems.
- The Context API can be used to share states across components without prop-drilling.
- Custom hooks allow you to extract stateful logic, making it reusable.
- This combination greatly improves the structure and readability of your code.

By adopting this approach, you'll have a much cleaner and more organized code, and you'll create a very scalable state management system. This combination is essential to master as you build increasingly complex applications.

4.3 REDUX VS. ZUSTAND VS. RECOIL: CHOOSING YOUR STATE MANAGEMENT ARSENAL

As your React applications grow in size and complexity, you may find that the built-in Context API isn't enough to handle your state management needs. This is where third-party state management libraries come into play, offering more advanced features and structured approaches to managing your application's state. We'll take a deep dive into three notable libraries: Redux, Zustand, and Recoil.

Redux: The Established and Structured Choice

Redux is a highly popular and widely used state management library in the React ecosystem. It's known for its structured and predictable approach, which makes it great for large-scale, complex applications. Redux implements a unidirectional data flow, meaning that data flows in a single direction. This is what makes it predictable and maintainable, but it also adds some complexity.

Key concepts in Redux:

- **Store:** The central place that holds the entire application state, it is the "single source of truth".
- **Actions:** Plain JavaScript objects that describe what happened in the application, they are the "events" that occur.
- **Reducers:** Pure functions that specify how the state changes in response to actions. Reducers are how we update our state.
- **Middleware:** Functions that intercept actions before they reach the reducers, used for logging, side effects, and other functionalities.

Redux in Action

Let's see how Redux is used in a React component. For this, you'll need the redux and react-redux packages.

First, let's define our actions:

actions.js:

```
export const INCREMENT = 'INCREMENT';
export const DECREMENT = 'DECREMENT';

export const increment = () => ({
  type: INCREMENT,
});

export const decrement = () => ({
  type: DECREMENT,
});
```

Here we are defining the constants for our actions.

Next, we must create our reducer.

reducer.js:

```
import { INCREMENT, DECREMENT } from './actions';

const initialState = {
```

```
    count: 0
};
function counterReducer(state = initialState, action){
    switch (action.type) {
        case INCREMENT:
            return {
                ...state,
                count: state.count + 1
            }
        case DECREMENT:
            return {
                ...state,
                count: state.count - 1
            }
        default:
            return state;
    }
}
export default counterReducer;
```

Here, we define our initial state for our store, as well as create our reducer that updates our state.

Next, we need to create our store:

store.js:

```
    import { createStore } from 'redux';
import counterReducer from './reducer';

const store = createStore(counterReducer);
export default store;
```

Here, we create a store using the createStore function, and pass in our reducer function that updates our state.

And finally, we create our component that uses our store:

MyComponent.js:

```
    import React from 'react';
import { useDispatch, useSelector } from 'react-redux';
import { increment, decrement } from './actions';
function MyComponent(){
    const count = useSelector(state => state.count);
```

```
    const dispatch = useDispatch();
    return (
        <div>
            <p>Count: {count}</p>
            <button onClick={() =>
dispatch(increment())}>Increment</button>
            <button onClick={() =>
dispatch(decrement())}>Decrement</button>
        </div>
    )
}
export default MyComponent;
```

Here we are using the hooks that the react-redux library provides us to interact with the store. useSelector allows us to get data from the store, and useDispatch allows us to update the store.

Lastly, let's provide the store with our App component:

```
import React from 'react';
import { Provider } from 'react-redux';
import store from './store';
import MyComponent from "./MyComponent";

function App() {
    return (
      <Provider store={store}>
        <MyComponent />
      </Provider>
    );
}
export default App;
```

Here we are using the Provider from react-redux to pass in the store, so that the child components have access to the store.

Here's a breakdown of our Redux setup:

- **Actions**: We define action creators, which are functions that returns a plain javascript object with the type.
- **Reducer**: This function defines how state should be updated.
- **Store**: This is the central storage of our data.
- **Component**: We use the useDispatch and useSelector hooks from react-redux to access the store and to update it.

As you can see, Redux requires a lot of boilerplate, especially for smaller applications.

Zustand: The Lightweight and Simple Alternative

Zustand is a lightweight and unopinionated state management library that offers a simpler approach than Redux. It is often a preferred choice for developers who are looking for a state management library that does not require the complexity of Redux.

Key features of Zustand:

- **Single Store:** State is stored in a single store, that is a custom hook.
- **Direct Updates:** State updates are done directly, without having to use reducers or actions.
- **Hooks-Based API:** Uses hooks for easy integration into React applications.
- **Simpler Syntax:** Requires less boilerplate than Redux and easier to setup.

Zustand in Action

Let's implement our previous example using Zustand.

For this, you'll need the zustand package.

First, create your store using the create function:

store.js:

```
import { create } from 'zustand';

const useCounterStore = create(set => ({
    count: 0,
    increment: () => set(state => ({ count: state.count + 1 })),
    decrement: () => set(state => ({ count: state.count - 1 })),
}));
export default useCounterStore;
```

As you can see this is much less code than Redux, and it is much easier to setup and use.

Here's what's happening:

- We use the create function to create our store.
- The store contains our count state, and the functions for incrementing and decrementing.
- We are updating the state directly using the set function.

Next, we have our component:

MyComponent.js:

```
import React from 'react';
import useCounterStore from "./store";

function MyComponent(){
  const { count, increment, decrement } = useCounterStore();
  return (
      <div>
          <p>Count: {count}</p>
          <button onClick={increment}>Increment</button>
          <button onClick={decrement}>Decrement</button>
      </div>
  )
}
export default MyComponent;
```

In this component, we are directly using our custom hook to access and modify the store.

Here's the breakdown:

- We use the create function from zustand to create our store.
- The useCounterStore is the custom hook that exposes our state, as well as setter functions.
- The component then uses the custom hook to access and update the store.

As you can see, zustand is much easier to set up than Redux, and it also has very similar functionality.

Recoil: A React-Centric and Fine-Grained Solution

Recoil is a state management library built by Meta, and it is more tailored to React. It offers a fine-grained approach with atoms and selectors, that is more integrated with React's concurrent features.

Key concepts of Recoil:

- **Atoms:** Independent pieces of state, that can be updated.
- **Selectors:** Pure functions that derive data from the state atoms. Selectors should be used when deriving complex state.
- **React Integration**: Built by the React team, and closely follows the way react manages state.

Recoil in Action

For this, you will need the recoil package.

First, we create our atoms that will store our state:

```
atoms.js:
    import { atom } from 'recoil';

export const countState = atom({
    key: 'countState',
    default: 0,
});
```

Next, our component that updates the state:

MyComponent.js:

```
    import React from 'react';
import { useRecoilState } from 'recoil';
import { countState } from './atoms';

function MyComponent() {
    const [count, setCount] = useRecoilState(countState);
    const increment = () => setCount(count + 1);
    const decrement = () => setCount(count - 1);
    return (
      <div>
        <p>Count: {count}</p>
        <button onClick={increment}>Increment</button>
        <button onClick={decrement}>Decrement</button>
      </div>
    );
}

export default MyComponent;
```

Lastly, we wrap the component with the RecoilRoot component, which acts as the provider for all atoms and selectors:

```
import React from 'react';
import { RecoilRoot } from 'recoil';
import MyComponent from "./MyComponent";

function App(){
    return (
      <RecoilRoot>
          <MyComponent />
      </RecoilRoot>
    )
}
export default App;
```

Here's what's happening:

- We created a file called atoms.js, which contains our countState atom that keeps track of our count.
- The component then uses the useRecoilState hook to access and modify the countState.
- And lastly, the App is wrapped by the RecoilRoot, which provides the atoms to the child components.

Choosing The Right Library

- **Redux:** Choose Redux if you're building large, complex applications with complex state management and require very strict state management.
- **Zustand:** Choose Zustand if you prefer a simple, lightweight solution without all the boilerplate of Redux.
- **Recoil:** Choose Recoil if you're seeking a React-centric library with fine-grained state updates.

Personal Insight

In my experience, I have found Redux to be extremely complex, and I have only used it when I have a very complicated project that requires strict unidirectional data flow. I prefer using Zustand because it's so simple, and has all the functionality that I would need. I have never used Recoil for a project.

Key Takeaways:

- Redux provides a structured, predictable approach suitable for large-scale applications but has a lot of boilerplate.
- Zustand is a simpler, lightweight solution, excellent for those seeking easier implementation and less boilerplate code.
- Recoil offers a React-centric approach with atoms and selectors that is very closely integrated into React.
- The best state management library is the one that best suits the needs of your project.

Understanding these three popular state management libraries is crucial, and you should pick the right library based on the needs of your application. Each of them has their own unique benefits, which you should consider when choosing.

4.4 BEST PRACTICES FOR STATE MANAGEMENT: CRAFTING ROBUST APPLICATIONS

Effective state management is crucial for the long-term success of your React projects. Without a solid strategy, your codebase can become a tangled web of state variables and update functions. By following best practices, you will be able to reduce potential issues and build scalable applications.

Start with Local State First

As we have discussed, local state is state that is managed within a component using the useState hook. You should always start with local state first and then move to global state when it's necessary. This approach has many benefits:

- **Simpler Components**: Components that manage their own state are easier to reason about, and they have less dependencies on other parts of your application.
- **Less Complexity**: By using local state first, you avoid the overhead of setting up a global state management solution if it isn't needed.
- **Improved Performance**: By keeping the state local to a component, you ensure that only that component re-renders when that state is updated, preventing unnecessary re-renders throughout the application.

Practical Example: Local State for Form Input

Let's take a look at an example using a form:

```
import React, { useState } from 'react';

function Form() {
  const [name, setName] = useState('');
  const [email, setEmail] = useState('');

  function handleNameChange(event) {
    setName(event.target.value);
  }
  function handleEmailChange(event) {
    setEmail(event.target.value);
  }

  return (
    <form>
        <label>
            Name:
            <input type="text" value={name}
onChange={handleNameChange} />
        </label>
        <label>
            Email:
            <input type="email" value={email}
onChange={handleEmailChange} />
        </label>
        <button>Submit</button>
    </form>
  );
}
export default Form;
```

In this example, we use useState to manage the form input values. The state is managed locally because it's only relevant to the form. This will be easier to maintain, and less error prone. If you are starting to build your application, then try to use local state for as long as you can, because this pattern is much easier to maintain.

Use Context Wisely

As we've seen, the Context API provides a way to share state between components, while avoiding prop-drilling. However, it's important to use the Context API for what it's intended to do.

- **Data that is shared:** Only put state into the context that is shared across multiple components in the application, such as a user's authentication status, or a theme.

- **Avoid volatile data**: You should avoid putting any volatile data such as form state into context, or state that is specific to a component, as this can cause many unnecessary re-renders throughout your application.
- **Small Contexts**: Make sure to avoid putting all of your data in a single context, as this can become difficult to manage. Keep your contexts focused for each specific use case.

Avoid Prop Drilling

Prop drilling is when you have to pass props down through multiple layers of nested components. This can cause performance issues, and can be very difficult to maintain. Using the Context API, or another state management library is a good way to get around this problem.

Practical Implementation: Avoiding Prop Drilling

Let's create an example where we avoid prop drilling, by using the Context API:

```
import React, { createContext, useContext } from 'react';

const UserContext = createContext(null);

function UserProvider({ children, user }) {
    return <UserContext.Provider
value={user}>{children}</UserContext.Provider>;
}

function useUser() {
    return useContext(UserContext);
}

function GrandParent() {
    return <Parent />;
}

function Parent() {
    return <Child />;
}

function Child() {
  const user = useUser();
    return <p>User: {user?.name}</p>;
}

function App() {
    const user = { name: "John Doe" };
    return (
```

```
        <UserProvider user={user}>
          <GrandParent />
        </UserProvider>
    );
}
export default App;
```

Here's what's happening:

- We are using the Context API to share the user object.
- The GrandParent, Parent, and Child component don't have to receive props from their parent component. The Child component has direct access to the state using the useUser hook.
- If we didn't use global state, we would have had to pass the props from the App component, to the GrandParent, to the Parent, and finally to the Child, making this code very difficult to maintain.

By avoiding prop-drilling, we make our applications easier to maintain, and more scalable.

Use Immutable Updates

When updating state in React, it's important to update the state immutably. This means that you create a new copy of the state, instead of directly modifying it. There are many benefits of using immutable updates, such as the ability to implement time-travel debugging, and preventing bugs due to state mutation.

- **For Objects**: Use the spread operator (...) or Object.assign() to create new copies of objects:

```
setObject(prevObject => ({ ...prevObject, someValue: newValue
}));
```

- **For Arrays**: Use slice, map, filter, or the spread operator to create new copies of arrays:

```
setArray(prevArray => [...prevArray, newItem]);
setArray(prevArray => prevArray.filter(item => item.id !== id));
```

Extract Logic to Hooks

85

As components get more complex, it can be very useful to extract logic from components into reusable custom hooks. This can include any state or logic that should be shared by multiple components.

- **Reusability:** This will make code much more reusable across components, as the logic is now in its own isolated hook.
- **Readability:** It will make your components much more readable, as they will be more focused on their responsibilities.
- **Maintainability:** Your application will become much more maintainable as the code will be more organized.

Practical Implementation: A Custom Fetch Hook

Here's an example of using a custom hook to extract a fetch request out of a component.

useFetch.js:

```
import { useState, useEffect } from 'react';
function useFetch(url) {
    const [data, setData] = useState(null);
    const [loading, setLoading] = useState(true);
    const [error, setError] = useState(null);

    useEffect(() => {
        async function fetchData() {
            try {
                const response = await fetch(url);
                if (!response.ok) {
                    throw new Error('Failed to fetch');
                }
                const json = await response.json();
                setData(json);
            } catch (err) {
                setError(err.message);
            } finally {
                setLoading(false);
            }
        }
        fetchData();
    }, [url]);
    return { data, loading, error };
}
export default useFetch;
```

content_copy download
Use code with caution.Jsx

86

MyComponent.js:

```
    import React from 'react';
import useFetch from "./useFetch";

function MyComponent({url}) {
    const { data, loading, error } = useFetch(url);

    if (loading) return <p>Loading...</p>;
    if (error) return <p>Error: {error}</p>;

    return (
        <div>
           {data &&  <p>Data: {data.title}</p>}
        </div>
    );
}
export default MyComponent;
```

In this implementation, our logic for fetching data is now in its own hook, and we can pass in any URL that we want. This simplifies our component, and also makes our fetch logic reusable.

Memoize When Necessary

As we discussed, using useMemo and useCallback are essential when dealing with complex computations or function props. These prevent unnecessary re-renders by caching the result or function.

Choose the Right Library

As we have discussed, choosing the right library for your project is essential.

- Redux: Use for very large applications with complex state and strict control over data flow.
- Zustand: Use for smaller projects that require a lightweight state management solution.
- Recoil: Use if you are building a large scale application that needs atomic and very fine-grained state management.

Personal Insight

As a React developer, I find that having a good strategy for state management is crucial for maintaining the sanity of your codebase. I always start with local state, only reaching for global state management when it is necessary. Whenever I find that my component is doing too much, I try to extract reusable logic into custom hooks.

Key Takeaways:

- Start with local state first, and move to global when it is needed.
- Use the Context API wisely, and only for shared state.
- Avoid Prop drilling, this will make your components much easier to maintain.
- Use immutable state updates to prevent bugs, and to allow time travel debugging.
- Extract code into custom hooks to improve code reusability.
- Use useMemo and useCallback to avoid unnecessary re-renders.
- Choose the right library for state management for the complexity of your application.

By following these best practices, you'll create a more organized, performant, and scalable React application. Being intentional and deliberate about your state management strategy is key for long term maintainability.

CHAPTER 5: DATA FETCHING AND API INTEGRATION

In modern web development, data is everything, and most applications will rely on communicating with servers to display data to the user. This chapter will guide you through the ins and outs of data fetching in React, from simple requests to complex data management strategies. You'll learn how to integrate your React application with backend APIs, manage asynchronous data, and handle real-time data with WebSockets.

5.1 FETCHING DATA WITH FETCH API AND AXIOS: THE FOUNDATION OF API INTEGRATION

In almost every real-world React application, you'll need to retrieve data from an external API. This is what allows your applications to be dynamic, instead of just having static content. To do this, React provides the Fetch API, and many third party libraries such as Axios provide similar, yet more feature rich approaches.

Fetch API: The Browser's Built-In Fetching Tool

The Fetch API is a built-in browser interface for making network requests. It's modern, versatile, and promises a more straightforward way to fetch resources. You don't need to install any third-party libraries to use it, it is already built into the browser.

Here's how you can use the Fetch API to make a GET request:

```
import React, { useState, useEffect } from 'react';

function FetchData() {
    const [data, setData] = useState(null);
    const [loading, setLoading] = useState(true);
    const [error, setError] = useState(null);
    const url = 'https://jsonplaceholder.typicode.com/todos/1';

    useEffect(() => {
        fetch(url)
            .then(response => {
                if (!response.ok) {
                    throw new Error(`HTTP Error: ${response.status}`)
```

```
        }
        return response.json()
    })
    .then(json => setData(json))
    .catch(err => setError(err.message))
    .finally(() => setLoading(false))
}, [url]);


  if (loading) return <p>Loading...</p>;
  if (error) return <p>Error: {error}</p>;
  if(!data) return <p>No data!</p>
return (
    <div>
        <h1>{data.title}</h1>
        <p>Completed: {data.completed ? "Yes" : "No"}</p>
    </div>
  );
}

export default FetchData;
```

Let's step through the code:

1. **State Initialization:** We initialize three state variables using the useState hook: data (to hold the fetched data), loading (to track whether data is being fetched), and error (to store any errors). We also have a url variable that holds the url that we are going to be fetching from.
2. **useEffect Hook:** We're using the useEffect hook, with url as a dependency, to trigger the fetch request when the component mounts.
3. **Fetch Request:** The fetch(url) function makes an HTTP request to the URL.
    o We use the first .then to get the response object and to check that the response code is valid using response.ok. If not we throw an error.
    o We then use the second .then to transform the response to json, which returns a promise of our data.
    o The .then(json => setData(json)) sets the data state when the json is returned.
    o If the fetch fails, we are going to use .catch, and set the error state.
    o Lastly, we use .finally which will be executed regardless of the success or failure of the fetch request, we are setting the loading state to false here, to notify the component that we are done loading.
4. **Conditional Rendering:** Lastly we are conditionally rendering our component based on the current loading and error state of the component.

Key Aspects of the Fetch API:

- **Promises:** The Fetch API relies on Promises, making asynchronous operations more manageable.
- **Response Handling**: You have to manually handle the response code, and parse the response to json, which can add complexity to your code.
- **Simple API**: It's built into the browser, making it easy to use without adding third party libraries.

Axios: A More Feature-Rich Alternative

Axios is a popular third-party library that provides an alternative way to make HTTP requests. It's known for its more user-friendly API and additional features.

To use Axios, you'll first need to install it: npm install axios.

Here's the equivalent code using Axios:

```
import React, { useState, useEffect } from 'react';
import axios from 'axios';

function FetchData() {
    const [data, setData] = useState(null);
    const [loading, setLoading] = useState(true);
    const [error, setError] = useState(null);
    const url = 'https://jsonplaceholder.typicode.com/todos/1';

    useEffect(() => {
        axios.get(url)
            .then(response => setData(response.data))
            .catch(err => setError(err.message))
            .finally(() => setLoading(false))
    }, [url]);
    if (loading) return <p>Loading...</p>;
    if (error) return <p>Error: {error}</p>;
    if(!data) return <p>No data!</p>
    return (
        <div>
            <h1>{data.title}</h1>
            <p>Completed: {data.completed ? "Yes" : "No"}</p>
        </div>
    );
}
export default FetchData;
```

Here's a breakdown:

1. **Import Axios:** We import Axios using import axios from 'axios';.
2. **Axios GET Request:** We make a GET request to the given url using axios.get(url), instead of the fetch function.
3. **Response Handling:** Axios automatically transforms JSON responses, so we don't have to use the .json() method. This can save you a lot of time and boilerplate when fetching data.
4. **Error Handling:** The .catch and .finally blocks are the same as our previous example.

Key Advantages of Axios:

- **Automatic JSON Transformation:** Automatically transforms JSON responses without explicitly calling .json().
- **Interceptors:** Allows you to intercept requests and responses, which is very useful for things like authentication.
- **Cancelable Requests:** Allows you to cancel requests, which can help with performance.
- **Better Error Handling:** Provides a much more intuitive way of managing errors.

Practical Implementation: Making a POST Request with Axios

Let's expand on our current implementation and make a POST request, so that you can see how it is different than a GET request:

```
import React, { useState } from 'react';
import axios from 'axios';

function PostData() {
  const [title, setTitle] = useState('');
  const [completed, setCompleted] = useState(false);
  const [data, setData] = useState(null);
  const [loading, setLoading] = useState(false);
  const [error, setError] = useState(null);
  const url = 'https://jsonplaceholder.typicode.com/todos';
  function handleSubmit(e) {
    e.preventDefault();
    setLoading(true);
    axios.post(url, {
      title: title,
      completed: completed
    })
    .then(response => setData(response.data))
    .catch(err => setError(err.message))
    .finally(() => setLoading(false));
```

```
    }

    return (
        <form onSubmit={handleSubmit}>
            <label>
                Title:
                <input type="text" value={title} onChange={(e) =>
setTitle(e.target.value)} />
            </label>
            <label>
                Completed:
                <input type="checkbox" value={completed}
onChange={(e) => setCompleted(e.target.checked)} />
            </label>
            <button type="submit" disabled={loading}>Submit</button>
            {loading && <p>Loading...</p>}
            {error && <p>Error: {error}</p>}
            {data && <p>Successfully created: {data.title}</p>}
        </form>
    );
}

export default PostData;
```

Let's explore the code, and note the differences between our previous GET request:

- **Form State:** We are using state to track the title and completed values, and we are using state to track loading, data, and error as well.
- **handleSubmit Function**: We are making the axios post request to the API.
    - Instead of using axios.get, we are using axios.post, and passing in the URL, as well as an object for the request body.
    - We also update our states based on the success or failure of the request.
- **Conditional Rendering:** We use conditional rendering to display our loading message, error message, and also if the post request was a success.

This example shows how to make a POST request using Axios, and also how to send a request body to the server.

Personal Insight

While the Fetch API is often sufficient for simple use cases, I usually find myself gravitating towards Axios due to its additional features and ease of use. The automatic JSON transformation and interceptor features save me a lot of time and boilerplate code. I also appreciate that the error handling is much more straight forward with Axios.

Key Takeaways:

- The Fetch API is a built-in browser interface for making network requests, that can be used if you don't want to use third party libraries.
- Axios is a third-party library that provides a more powerful and easier-to-use API for making network requests, as well as additional features.
- Both the Fetch API and Axios rely on promises, and use similar logic to handle them.
- You should carefully consider whether you need the features that Axios provides, before deciding which library to use.

With a firm understanding of the Fetch API and Axios, you're now well-equipped to start fetching data in your React applications. These are the essential skills for any React developer.

5.2 REACT QUERY FOR OPTIMIZED DATA MANAGEMENT: A DEEP DIVE

React Query, now part of TanStack, is a library designed to solve common problems when fetching data in React applications. Instead of writing your own solutions for caching, managing loading states, and re-fetching, you can rely on React Query to do all of this for you. It streamlines data fetching, reduces boilerplate, and provides a much better user experience by handling many of the common issues that you'd encounter.

Understanding the Philosophy of React Query

At its heart, React Query treats data fetching as a declarative process, focusing on what data your component needs, rather than how the data is fetched. This approach simplifies data fetching operations by taking care of the most common concerns for you.

- **Queries**: React Query treats fetching data as a query, with the data cached using a unique key.
- **Mutations**: When data needs to be updated, you use mutations that update both the server, and also the cached value.

- **Automatic Caching**: Data is automatically cached based on its queryKey, reducing unnecessary requests and improving performance.
- **Stale-While-Revalidate**: Data is displayed immediately from the cache, while also updating the data in the background.
- **Hooks-Based**: Uses React hooks to provide an easy to use API.

Setting Up React Query

First, you need to install the library: npm install @tanstack/react-query.

Then, you need to set up the QueryClient and wrap your root component with the QueryClientProvider.

Here's how you'd typically do it in main.jsx or index.js:

```
import React from 'react';
import ReactDOM from 'react-dom/client';
import App from './App.jsx';
import { QueryClient, QueryClientProvider } from '@tanstack/react-query';

const queryClient = new QueryClient();

ReactDOM.createRoot(document.getElementById('root')).render(
  <React.StrictMode>
    <QueryClientProvider client={queryClient}>
      <App />
    </QueryClientProvider>
  </React.StrictMode>
);
```

Here's what's happening:

- We are importing the required functions from @tanstack/react-query.
- We're creating a new QueryClient instance, which will manage the state, caching and refetching of data throughout the application.
- We are wrapping our App in the QueryClientProvider component, which provides our components with access to the QueryClient.

With this setup, you are now ready to use React Query in your application.

Fetching Data with useQuery

The useQuery hook is where you'll be spending most of your time when working with React Query. It's used for fetching data and managing the state of that query.

Here's how you would fetch data and display it on the screen:

```
import React from 'react';
import { useQuery } from '@tanstack/react-query';
import axios from 'axios';

function FetchData() {
    const url = 'https://jsonplaceholder.typicode.com/todos/1';
    const { data, isLoading, error } = useQuery({
      queryKey: ['todos'],
        queryFn: async () => {
          const res = await axios.get(url);
          return res.data;
      }
    });
    if (isLoading) return <p>Loading...</p>;
    if (error) return <p>Error: {error.message}</p>;
    if(!data) return <p>No Data!</p>

    return (
        <div>
            <h1>{data.title}</h1>
            <p>Completed: {data.completed ? "Yes" : "No"}</p>
        </div>
    );
}
export default FetchData;
```

Let's go through the code:

- We import the useQuery hook from @tanstack/react-query as well as axios.
- We use the useQuery hook and pass it an options object with two main properties:
    - queryKey: The query key is a unique identifier for your query, and React Query will use this key to store data in the cache.
    - queryFn: This function is how we will be fetching the data. This function can be synchronous or asynchronous, and must return a promise of the data. In our case, we're using Axios to make a GET request to our endpoint.
- The useQuery hook will return to us a few properties that we can use, which includes data, isLoading, and error.

- o data: The fetched data, which will initially be undefined when the component first renders.
  - o isLoading: Will be true when data is being fetched, and false otherwise.
  - o error: If there was an error during the request, this will contain the error.
- We then use this information to conditionally render the component based on the data.

Key Benefits of useQuery:

- **Automatic State Management**: Handles loading, error states, and data management.
- **Caching**: Caches fetched data based on its queryKey.
- **Stale-While-Revalidate**: Provides cached data immediately while also updating in the background.
- **Simplified Data Fetching**: Allows us to focus on the application's user interface instead of the complexity of data fetching.

Updating Data with useMutation

When you need to update, create or delete data on the server, you should use the useMutation hook. This hook handles updating data on the server, and also manages updating the cache.

Here's an example using a POST request, to create a new resource:

```
import React, { useState } from 'react';
import { useMutation } from '@tanstack/react-query';
import axios from 'axios';

function PostData() {
    const [title, setTitle] = useState('');
    const [completed, setCompleted] = useState(false);
    const url = 'https://jsonplaceholder.typicode.com/todos';

    const mutation = useMutation({
        mutationFn: (newTodo) => {
            return axios.post(url, newTodo)
                .then(response => response.data)
        }
    });
  function handleSubmit(e) {
    e.preventDefault();
    mutation.mutate({
```

```
        title: title,
        completed: completed
    });
  }
    if (mutation.isLoading) return <p>Loading...</p>;
    if (mutation.isError) return <p>Error:
{mutation.error.message}</p>;
    if (mutation.isSuccess) return <p>Successfully created:
{mutation.data.title}</p>;
  return (
    <form onSubmit={handleSubmit}>
        <label>
          Title:
          <input type="text" value={title} onChange={(e) =>
setTitle(e.target.value)} />
      </label>
        <label>
          Completed:
          <input type="checkbox" value={completed} onChange={(e)
=> setCompleted(e.target.checked)} />
        </label>
        <button type="submit"
disabled={mutation.isLoading}>Submit</button>
    </form>
    );
}
export default PostData;
```

Let's go through this code:

- We are importing the useMutation hook from @tanstack/react-query as well as axios.
- We use the useMutation hook, and pass in an options object with a mutationFn property.
  - mutationFn is a function that will make the API call, and returns a promise containing the data from the API.
- We call the mutation.mutate function in our handleSubmit, and we pass it the data that we want to send to the server.
- We use isLoading, isError, and isSuccess to conditionally render our component.

Key Benefits of useMutation:

- **Simplified Data Updating**: Handles all the complexity of updating data on the server and updating your cache in the background.

- **Automatic State Management**: Tracks loading states and errors during mutation.
- **Cache Invalidation**: Automatically updates the cache based on successful mutations.

Practical Implementation: Fetching a List of Items with Pagination

Let's make a more complex example, where we are using React Query to fetch a list of items, and implement pagination:

```
import React, { useState } from 'react';
import { useQuery } from '@tanstack/react-query';
import axios from 'axios';

function FetchData() {
    const [page, setPage] = useState(1);
    const url =
`https://jsonplaceholder.typicode.com/todos?_page=${page}&_limit=5`
;
    const { data, isLoading, error, isPreviousData } = useQuery({
        queryKey: ['todos', page],
        queryFn: () => axios.get(url).then(res => res.data),
        keepPreviousData: true,
    });
  function handlePrevPage() {
    setPage(prevPage => Math.max(prevPage - 1, 1));
  }
  function handleNextPage() {
      setPage(prevPage => prevPage + 1)
  }
  if(isLoading) return <p>Loading...</p>
    if(error) return <p>Error: {error.message}</p>
    if (!data) return <p>No Data!</p>;
    return (
        <div>
            <h1>Todos</h1>
            <ul>
                {data.map(todo => (
                    <li key={todo.id}>{todo.title}</li>
                ))}
            </ul>
            <button disabled={page === 1}
onClick={handlePrevPage}>Previous</button>
            <button disabled={isPreviousData}
onClick={handleNextPage}>Next</button>
            <p>Page: {page}</p>
        </div>
    );
}
```

```
export default FetchData;
```

Here's a breakdown:

- We are using our useQuery to fetch a list of todos from our API.
- We are passing in page as a dependency to the queryKey, to make sure that the data that is cached is specific to the page that we are looking at.
- We are also passing in keepPreviousData to keep the old data, and to transition to the new data smoothly.
- We also handle our previous and next page buttons using some local state.
- We use isPreviousData to know if we are on the previous page.

This example demonstrates that React Query is not only simple to use, but also scales very well to more complex scenarios.

Personal Insights

React Query has transformed the way I handle data fetching. Before, I was used to writing code to manage caching, state, and background updates. Now with react query, I can focus solely on the user experience, and React Query does the rest. If your application is handling a lot of server side data, I highly recommend that you look into React Query.

Key Takeaways:

- React Query is a fantastic library for data management in React that reduces boilerplate code.
- useQuery is used to fetch and cache data, providing built in state management.
- useMutation is used to make updates on the server and manages cache updates.
- React Query handles all of the loading states, caching, and errors out of the box.

By understanding how to use React Query, you'll be able to build more robust, efficient, and maintainable React applications. These skills are essential for handling asynchronous data in modern applications.

5.3 HANDLING LOADING, ERRORS, AND CACHING: ESSENTIAL PRACTICES FOR DATA FETCHING

When you're working with asynchronous data in React, you need to handle different scenarios gracefully. Users should be aware of when data is loading, informed when there are errors, and you should also implement caching to avoid sending unnecessary requests. Without good practices for loading, error and caching, your application might feel slow and unreliable.

Loading States: Providing Feedback to the User

Loading states are crucial for providing feedback to users when data is being fetched. Without a loading indicator, users might think that your application is broken, or that something isn't working. It helps manage user expectations by showing that something is happening.

Let's look at an example using the built in fetch API:

```
import React, { useState, useEffect } from 'react';

function LoadingState() {
    const [data, setData] = useState(null);
    const [loading, setLoading] = useState(true);
    const [error, setError] = useState(null);
    const url = 'https://jsonplaceholder.typicode.com/todos/1';

    useEffect(() => {
        fetch(url)
            .then(response => {
                if (!response.ok) {
                    throw new Error(`HTTP Error:
${response.status}`)
                }
                return response.json();
            })
            .then(json => setData(json))
            .catch(err => setError(err.message))
            .finally(() => setLoading(false));
    }, [url]);
    if (loading) return <p>Loading...</p>;
    if (error) return <p>Error: {error}</p>;
    if (!data) return <p>No Data!</p>;
    return (
```

```
        <div>
            <h1>{data.title}</h1>
            <p>Completed: {data.completed ? "Yes" : "No"}</p>
        </div>
    );
}
export default LoadingState;
```

Let's break this example down:

- We use the useState hook to track the loading state, initialized as true.
- During our fetch request, we are using .finally to set the loading state to false, regardless of whether the request was successful or not.
- We are conditionally rendering our component based on the current value of loading, by showing a Loading... message while loading is true.

Here, we are using a simple paragraph to display a loading message, but in most real-world applications, you will be using some more complex loading indicators.

Error Handling: Informing Users and Debugging Issues

When things go wrong with a fetch request, it is important to inform users about the error, and also provide a way to debug the error. Proper error handling not only makes your application more reliable, it helps improve the user experience.

Let's look at the previous example again, but this time also focus on error handling:

```
        import React, { useState, useEffect } from 'react';

function ErrorState() {
    const [data, setData] = useState(null);
    const [loading, setLoading] = useState(true);
    const [error, setError] = useState(null);
    const url = 'https://jsonplaceholder.typicode.com/todos/1';

    useEffect(() => {
        fetch(url)
            .then(response => {
                if (!response.ok) {
                    throw new Error(`HTTP Error:
${response.status}`)
                }
                return response.json();
            })
            .then(json => setData(json))
```

```
            .catch(err => setError(err.message))
            .finally(() => setLoading(false));
    }, [url]);
    if (loading) return <p>Loading...</p>;
    if (error) return <p>Error: {error}</p>;
    if(!data) return <p>No Data!</p>
    return (
        <div>
            <h1>{data.title}</h1>
            <p>Completed: {data.completed ? "Yes" : "No"}</p>
        </div>
    );
}
export default ErrorState;
```

Here's how error handling is implemented:

- We are using our useState hook to create a state for our error message, error.
- We have introduced error handling in our fetch request using .catch, and setting our error message when there is an error.
- We are conditionally rendering based on whether there is an error, and displaying an error message to the user.

In a real-world application, you will also be using a tool to log the error, such as using console.error, or a logging tool to log this error to the server, so that you can debug it.

Caching: Reducing API Requests

Caching is a technique that stores previously fetched data, so that it can be reused again if the data has not changed. Caching drastically improves your application's performance, as it avoids having to send unnecessary API requests, saving time and bandwidth.

There are many caching strategies:

- **In-Memory Cache**: Data is cached in the application's memory, usually in a state variable. This cache is only available for the current session.
- **Browser Storage**: Data can be stored in the browser's local storage or session storage.
- **Server-Side Cache**: Data is cached on the server.
- **CDN**: Data can also be stored in a CDN.

Let's take a look at how you can implement caching using the sessionStorage api:

```jsx
import React, { useState, useEffect } from 'react';

function CacheState() {
    const [data, setData] = useState(null);
    const [loading, setLoading] = useState(true);
    const [error, setError] = useState(null);
    const url = 'https://jsonplaceholder.typicode.com/todos/1';

    useEffect(() => {
        const cachedData = sessionStorage.getItem(url);
        if (cachedData) {
            setData(JSON.parse(cachedData));
            setLoading(false);
            return;
        }
        fetch(url)
            .then(response => {
                if (!response.ok) {
                    throw new Error(`HTTP Error: ${response.status}`)
                }
                return response.json()
            })
            .then(json => {
                setData(json);
                sessionStorage.setItem(url, JSON.stringify(json));
            })
            .catch(err => setError(err.message))
            .finally(() => setLoading(false))
    }, [url]);
    if (loading) return <p>Loading...</p>;
    if (error) return <p>Error: {error}</p>;
    if (!data) return <p>No data!</p>
    return (
        <div>
            <h1>{data.title}</h1>
            <p>Completed: {data.completed ? "Yes" : "No"}</p>
        </div>
    );
}
export default CacheState;
```

Here's how the caching is implemented:

- First we check sessionStorage to see if there is already data available. If there is, we are going to parse the data and set the component's state.

- If there isn't any data in sessionStorage, then we are going to fetch the data and then store that value into the sessionStorage for next time.
- We are also handling our loading and error states as we have done previously.

As you can see, implementing caching yourself can be tricky, and can often result in bugs that are hard to debug. This is why we recommend using a third-party library such as React Query to manage our state for us.

Using React Query for Loading, Errors and Caching

As we've discussed, React Query provides a more simplified and robust way of managing our loading, errors, and caching. React Query manages the data by using a queryKey, that can be used to store data for an extended period of time. It also manages the loading state and error state, which helps to simplify the code that you need to write.

Here's how you can use React Query to fetch data and manage all these states:

```
import React from 'react';
import { useQuery } from '@tanstack/react-query';
import axios from 'axios';

function ReactQueryState() {
    const url = 'https://jsonplaceholder.typicode.com/todos/1';
    const { data, isLoading, error } = useQuery({
        queryKey: ['todos'],
        queryFn: () => axios.get(url).then(res => res.data),
    });
    if (isLoading) return <p>Loading...</p>;
    if (error) return <p>Error: {error.message}</p>;
    if(!data) return <p>No data!</p>
    return (
        <div>
            <h1>{data.title}</h1>
            <p>Completed: {data.completed ? "Yes" : "No"}</p>
        </div>
    );
}
export default ReactQueryState;
```

Here's a breakdown of the code:

- We are using the useQuery hook from @tanstack/react-query to fetch the data.
- The queryKey is what we are using to uniquely identify our request, this is also used by React Query to store the data in the cache.
- The queryFn is the function that is used to make the request.
- We are using the isLoading, error, and data to render our component conditionally.

With this implementation, React Query is handling loading, errors, and caching for us automatically.

Personal Insight

When I first started building React applications, I found that handling loading, errors, and caching required a lot of manual work, and I often introduced bugs into my code. When I discovered React Query I found that it significantly reduced the boilerplate code, and also helped to make my applications more performant. This is why I highly recommend React Query for managing all of your state.

Key Takeaways:

- Loading states provide valuable feedback to the user when data is being fetched from the server.
- Proper error handling is necessary to provide a more reliable user experience.
- Caching can improve the performance of your application by avoiding unnecessary API calls.
- React Query provides a very robust way of managing all the loading, error, and caching states in a very simple and efficient manner.

By mastering these practices, you'll be able to create React applications that are both performant and reliable, and will provide a great experience to your users. This is essential when building any React application.

5.4 WEBSOCKETS AND REAL-TIME DATA IN REACT: BUILDING INTERACTIVE EXPERIENCES

In many modern web applications, you need to display data that is constantly being updated. This could be a chat application, live sports results, or a stock market dashboard. Traditional methods using HTTP requests are not suitable for real-time data, as they only send data on request, which is why WebSockets are essential in these situations. WebSockets provide a persistent, bidirectional connection between client and server, allowing data to be pushed from server to client in real-time. This provides a truly interactive experience for the end users.

Understanding the WebSocket Protocol

Unlike HTTP requests, WebSockets establish a continuous connection. Once a connection is established, both the client and the server can send and receive messages at any time, without needing to constantly request new data.

Key characteristics of WebSockets:

- **Persistent Connection**: Maintains an open connection for real-time communication.
- **Bidirectional Communication**: Data can be sent and received by both the client and the server.
- **Low Latency**: Offers low latency communication, enabling rapid updates.
- **Efficient Communication**: Reduced overhead compared to HTTP polling.

Setting up a WebSocket Connection in React

Let's look at the basic steps for setting up a WebSocket connection in React.

```
import React, { useState, useEffect } from 'react';
function WebSocketComponent() {
  const [message, setMessage] = useState('');
  const socketUrl = 'wss://echo.websocket.events';
  useEffect(() => {
    const socket = new WebSocket(socketUrl);
      socket.onopen = () => console.log('WebSocket connected.');
    socket.onmessage = (event) => setMessage(event.data);
    socket.onclose = () => console.log("WebSocket disconnected.");
    socket.onerror = (error) => console.log("WebSocket Error:", error)
        return () => {
          socket.close();
        };
  }, []);

  return (
      <div>
          <p>Real-Time Message: {message}</p>
      </div>
  );
}
```

```
export default WebSocketComponent;
```

Here's a step-by-step explanation:

1. **State Initialization:** We are using the useState hook to store the messages we receive from the server, by initializing the state with an empty string.
2. **useEffect Hook:** We're using the useEffect hook to manage our connection, and all of the event handlers. The dependency array is empty, so this effect will only run when the component is mounted.
   - **Creating a WebSocket Connection:** We create a new WebSocket connection, using the URL of the server.
   - **Event Handlers:** We are attaching event listeners for the onopen, onmessage, onclose, and onerror events. Each of these event handlers is used to log the event in the console.
   - **Closing the Connection:** We are also using the return statement from the useEffect to close the WebSocket connection when the component unmounts.
3. **Display Message**: Lastly we are displaying the messages on the screen.

In this example, we are connecting to a WebSocket echo server, and whenever we send a message, the server will send it back to us, which is then displayed in the UI.

Sending Messages with WebSockets

Let's expand on the previous example, and create a form where users can type a message, and send it to the server using the WebSocket connection.

```
import React, { useState, useEffect } from 'react';

function WebSocketComponent() {
  const [message, setMessage] = useState('');
    const [inputValue, setInputValue] = useState("");
  const socketUrl = 'wss://echo.websocket.events';
    const [socket, setSocket] = useState(null);

  useEffect(() => {
      const socket = new WebSocket(socketUrl);
      setSocket(socket);
      socket.onopen = () => console.log('WebSocket connected.');
      socket.onmessage = (event) => setMessage(event.data);
      socket.onclose = () => console.log("WebSocket
disconnected.");
      socket.onerror = (error) => console.log("WebSocket Error:",
error)
```

```
      return () => {
        socket.close();
      };
  }, []);
  function handleSubmit(e){
    e.preventDefault();
    if(socket && socket.readyState === WebSocket.OPEN){
        socket.send(inputValue)
        setInputValue("");
    } else {
        console.log("Socket not connected")
    }
  }

    return (
      <div>
        <p>Real-Time Message: {message}</p>
        <form onSubmit={handleSubmit}>
            <input type="text" value={inputValue} onChange={(e)
=> setInputValue(e.target.value)} />
            <button type="submit">Send Message</button>
        </form>
      </div>
    );
}
export default WebSocketComponent;
```

Here's how we are sending messages:

- We are now storing the WebSocket object into a state variable socket.
- We are also using the inputValue state to store the value from the text field.
- We are creating a handleSubmit function, that sends the message using the socket.send() function.
- We are using our input's onChange function to store the value of the input, into our inputValue state.
- We are only sending the message if the socket is opened, otherwise we are going to display an error in the console.

This expanded example allows you to send messages and display the responses in real time.

Implementing a Chat Application with WebSockets

Let's implement a basic chat application where you can send and receive messages in real time:

```jsx
import React, { useState, useEffect } from 'react';

function ChatApp() {
    const [messages, setMessages] = useState([]);
    const [inputValue, setInputValue] = useState('');
    const socketUrl = 'wss://echo.websocket.events';
    const [socket, setSocket] = useState(null);

    useEffect(() => {
        const socket = new WebSocket(socketUrl);
        setSocket(socket);
        socket.onopen = () => console.log('WebSocket connected.');
        socket.onmessage = (event) => setMessages(prevMessages =>
[...prevMessages, { text: event.data, isMe: false }]);
        socket.onclose = () => console.log("WebSocket
disconnected.");
        socket.onerror = (error) => console.log("WebSocket Error:",
error);
      return () => {
          socket.close();
      };
    }, []);
    function handleSubmit(e) {
        e.preventDefault();
        if (socket && socket.readyState === WebSocket.OPEN) {
            socket.send(inputValue);
            setMessages(prevMessages => [...prevMessages, { text:
inputValue, isMe: true }]);
            setInputValue('');
        } else {
            console.log("Socket not connected");
        }
    }
    return (
        <div>
            <div>
                {messages.map((message, index) => (
                    <div key={index} style={{ textAlign:
message.isMe ? 'right' : 'left' }}>
                        <p>{message.text}</p>
                    </div>
                ))}
            </div>
             <form onSubmit={handleSubmit}>
                <input type="text" value={inputValue} onChange={(e)
=> setInputValue(e.target.value)} />
                <button type="submit">Send Message</button>
            </form>
        </div>
    );
}
```

```
export default ChatApp;
```

Here's how our chat application is implemented:

- We now have a messages array to hold all messages, which are an object with a text property, and an isMe boolean.
- When a message is received, the onmessage event listener will add a new message object with the text and isMe set to false.
- When the user submits the form, we will send the message, and also update the messages array with isMe set to true.
- Lastly we are mapping over the messages and displaying them.

With this example, you have a fully functioning chat application that displays messages in real time.

Personal Insight

I still remember how difficult it was for me to implement a chat application before I knew about WebSockets. I had to use polling, which was extremely slow and inefficient. When I discovered WebSockets, it completely changed my approach, and allowed me to build interactive applications without all the boilerplate.

Key Takeaways:

- WebSockets provide a persistent, bidirectional connection between the client and server.
- They are used when real time data is needed.
- You can use the WebSocket API to connect to a WebSocket server.
- WebSockets enable you to send messages back and forth in real time, allowing you to build interactive applications such as chat apps.

By understanding WebSockets, you'll be able to build real-time applications that are interactive and engaging. This is a very valuable skill to have, as many modern web applications rely on real time communication.

CHAPTER 6: ROUTING WITH REACT ROUTER 7

In single-page applications (SPAs), client-side routing is essential for managing different views and navigating between them. React Router is the most popular library for handling routing in React applications. This chapter will be your comprehensive guide to using React Router 7, the latest version of this popular library.

6.1 SETTING UP CLIENT-SIDE ROUTING: THE BASICS OF NAVIGATION

In a single-page application, client-side routing is the mechanism that allows users to navigate between different views or pages, without requiring a full page reload. React Router is the most popular library for handling routing in React. It provides the essential tools and features for setting up navigation, and allows you to create a single page application that is scalable and well organized.

Why Client-Side Routing?

In traditional web applications, the server is responsible for sending the correct HTML to a browser when navigating to different pages. In React, all rendering is done on the client side. This gives you a much faster and more interactive experience, but we will need a way for users to navigate to different parts of the application, hence client-side routing.

Installing React Router

First, you need to install React Router using npm:

```
npm install react-router-dom@7
```

Make sure you install react-router-dom@7 because the APIs are different in older versions of the library.

Core Components of React Router

React Router provides several key components that you'll be using to set up routing in your applications:

- **BrowserRouter**: This is a router component that uses the browser's history API to keep track of all the routes that the user is navigating through. This is the main router that you will be using for your single page application, and all routing logic will need to be wrapped inside this router.
- **Routes**: This component acts as a container for the route definitions. It will render the first route that matches the current URL that the user has navigated to.
- **Route**: This component is used to define the route. Each Route component will have a path, which is the path that the route will match, and an element property which contains the component that will be rendered.
- **Link**: This component is used to navigate to a specific route in the application, similar to an <a> element, but it prevents a page reload, instead, it just updates the URL and renders the new component.

Implementing a Basic Routing System

Let's set up a basic example, where we are going to create a few routes, including a home page, an about page, and a contact page.

```
import React from 'react';
import { BrowserRouter, Routes, Route, Link } from 'react-router-dom';

function Home() {
  return <h1>Home Page</h1>;
}

function About() {
  return <h1>About Page</h1>;
}

function Contact() {
  return <h1>Contact Page</h1>;
}

function App() {
  return (
    <BrowserRouter>
      <nav>
        <ul>
          <li><Link to="/">Home</Link></li>
```

```
      <li><Link to="/about">About</Link></li>
      <li><Link to="/contact">Contact</Link></li>
    </ul>
  </nav>
  <Routes>
    <Route path="/" element={<Home />} />
    <Route path="/about" element={<About />} />
    <Route path="/contact" element={<Contact />} />
  </Routes>
</BrowserRouter>
);
}

export default App;
```

Let's walk through the code step by step:

1. **Importing Components:** We import the components from the react-router-dom library. We also import the components that we want to render for each of our routes.
2. **BrowserRouter:** We are wrapping our application with the BrowserRouter, which will provide our application with the client side routing capabilities.
3. **Navigation Links:** We are creating navigation links using the Link components. The to prop is used to specify the path that you want to link to.
4. **Routes Component:** We're using the Routes component to wrap our route definitions.
5. **Route Components:** Inside our Routes, we have our route definitions. Each Route has two key properties:
   o path: This is the path that will be matched by this route.
   o element: This is the component that will be rendered when the path is matched.
6. **Rendering the Components**: We are rendering the components based on the current route.

By creating the components and rendering them using React Router, you have successfully created a basic routing system in your application. If you click on any of the links, you can see that the URL in your browser updates, without causing a full page reload.

Practical Implementation: Adding a 404 Page

Let's expand on this example and create a 404 page, so that when a user navigates to a page that does not exist, it is gracefully handled, instead of crashing your application.

```
import React from 'react';
import { BrowserRouter, Routes, Route, Link } from 'react-router-dom';

function Home() {
  return <h1>Home Page</h1>;
}

function About() {
  return <h1>About Page</h1>;
}

function Contact() {
  return <h1>Contact Page</h1>;
}

function NotFound() {
    return <h1>404: Page not found</h1>
}
function App() {
  return (
    <BrowserRouter>
      <nav>
        <ul>
          <li><Link to="/">Home</Link></li>
          <li><Link to="/about">About</Link></li>
          <li><Link to="/contact">Contact</Link></li>
        </ul>
      </nav>
      <Routes>
        <Route path="/" element={<Home />} />
        <Route path="/about" element={<About />} />
        <Route path="/contact" element={<Contact />} />
        <Route path="*" element={<NotFound />} />
      </Routes>
    </BrowserRouter>
  );
}

export default App;
```

Here, we are using the wildcard * to match any URL that was not previously defined. If any of the previously defined URLs match the current URL, then the corresponding component will be rendered. If none of them match, then the 404 component will be rendered.

Personal Insight

When I first started learning React, I wasn't sure why we needed a routing system, but after building several applications, I realized how crucial it was for creating a single page application. React Router provides all the necessary tools to build complex, multi page applications, and allows you to seamlessly navigate to different parts of your application without the page reloading.

Key Takeaways:

- Client-side routing enables navigation within a single-page application without a full page reload.
- React Router is the most popular and commonly used library for client-side routing in React.
- You will need to use the BrowserRouter component to enable client side routing for your application.
- The Routes and Route components are used to define the route definitions, including the URL, and the component that will be rendered.
- The Link components are used to navigate to different routes.
- You can use the wildcard * to match any URL, and render a 404 page.

By understanding how to set up client-side routing, you have laid the foundation for building more complex, multi-page applications with React. This is the essential skill that you will need to master before moving onto more advanced topics.

6.2 DYNAMIC AND NESTED ROUTES: BUILDING MORE COMPLEX APPLICATIONS

While basic routing using fixed paths and components is good for simple applications, most applications will require more dynamic behavior. Dynamic routes allow you to create routes with parameters, enabling you to display data based on a specific identifier. Nested routes are used to create hierarchical layouts, providing a structured and organized way to manage navigation.

Dynamic Routes: Using Parameters in URLs

Dynamic routes involve URL paths with parameters, allowing you to create a single route that matches various URLs based on identifiers. This is essential when you have to display pages based on a data ID.

Let's see a practical example of how to implement dynamic routing in React Router, where we are going to create a component that displays information about a single product.

```
import React from 'react';
import { BrowserRouter, Routes, Route, Link, useParams } from
'react-router-dom';

const products = [
    { id: 1, name: 'Product 1', description: 'Description 1' },
    { id: 2, name: 'Product 2', description: 'Description 2' },
    { id: 3, name: 'Product 3', description: 'Description 3' },
];

function Product() {
    const { id } = useParams();
    const product = products.find(p => p.id === parseInt(id));
    if (!product) return <p>Product not found</p>;
    return (
        <div>
            <h1>{product.name}</h1>
            <p>{product.description}</p>
        </div>
    );
}
function ProductList() {
    return (
        <div>
            <h1>Products</h1>
            <ul>
              {products.map(product => (
                <li key={product.id}>
                    <Link
to={`/products/${product.id}`}>{product.name}</Link>
                </li>
              ))}
            </ul>
        </div>
    );
}

function App() {
    return (
        <BrowserRouter>
            <nav>
```

```
        <ul>
          <li><Link to="/">Home</Link></li>
          <li><Link to="/products">Products</Link></li>
        </ul>
      </nav>
      <Routes>
        <Route path="/" element={<h1>Home Page</h1>} />
        <Route path="/products" element={<ProductList />} />
        <Route path="/products/:id" element={<Product />} />
      </Routes>
    </BrowserRouter>
  );
}
export default App;
```

Let's go through the code step by step:

1. **Importing Components:** We import the useParams hook from the react-router-dom library, as well as the required routing components.
2. **useParams Hook:** We use the useParams hook inside of our Product component to access the parameters that are passed into the route. For our case, we are using the id param, that we have defined in our route.
3. **Dynamic Route Path:** In our Routes component, we define the path as /products/:id, where the :id is a dynamic parameter. This means that any path that matches /products/ and then any identifier after it will be rendered by the /products/:id route.
4. **Finding the product**: In the product component, we are using the id to find a product from our products array. If the product does not exist, then a message saying that it does not exist will be displayed.
5. **Linking to products**: In the ProductList component, we are using the Link components to navigate to our individual product pages using the dynamic routes.

By using dynamic routes, you can handle many different URLs with a single route. This allows you to build more dynamic applications with less code.

Nested Routes: Organizing Hierarchical Content

Nested routes allow you to organize your application's content using hierarchical layouts, that are essential for building more complex UIs. This gives you a cleaner more structured way of building your UI.

Let's take a look at how you can implement nested routes, in a dashboard example.

```jsx
    import React from 'react';
import { BrowserRouter, Routes, Route, Link, Outlet } from 'react-
router-dom';

function DashboardLayout() {
    return (
        <div>
            <h1>Dashboard</h1>
             <nav>
                <Link to="/dashboard/settings">Settings</Link>
                <Link to="/dashboard/analytics">Analytics</Link>
            </nav>
             <Outlet />
        </div>
    );
}

function DashboardSettings() {
  return <h1>Dashboard Settings</h1>;
}
function DashboardAnalytics() {
    return <h1>Dashboard Analytics</h1>;
}
function App() {
    return (
        <BrowserRouter>
            <nav>
              <ul>
                <li><Link to="/">Home</Link></li>
                <li><Link to="/dashboard">Dashboard</Link></li>
              </ul>
            </nav>
            <Routes>
                <Route path="/" element={<h1>Home Page</h1>} />
                <Route path="/dashboard" element={<DashboardLayout
/>}>
                    <Route path="settings" element={<DashboardSettings
/>} />
                    <Route path="analytics"
element={<DashboardAnalytics />} />
                </Route>
            </Routes>
        </BrowserRouter>
    );
}
export default App;
```

Here's a breakdown:

1. **Importing Components:** We are importing the required components from react-router-dom.
2. **Outlet Component:** The Outlet component is used to render the child routes of a parent route. This is the most essential component for nesting routes, as this renders child components.
3. **Nested Route Definitions:** We are defining the /dashboard route, which is the parent route, and then nested within that route are the settings and analytics routes.
4. **Child Components:** The DashboardSettings and DashboardAnalytics components are the components that are rendered at their respective paths, within the DashboardLayout.

When a user visits /dashboard/settings, then the DashboardLayout will be rendered, and the DashboardSettings component will be rendered inside the Outlet of that component.

Practical Implementation: Combining Dynamic and Nested Routes

Let's expand our example, and combine dynamic and nested routes. We're going to create a page where we display a list of products, and then when we click the product we go to a specific product page, and then we can also go to a specific products reviews page.

```
import React from 'react';
import { BrowserRouter, Routes, Route, Link, useParams, Outlet }
from 'react-router-dom';

const products = [
    { id: 1, name: 'Product 1', description: 'Description 1' },
    { id: 2, name: 'Product 2', description: 'Description 2' },
    { id: 3, name: 'Product 3', description: 'Description 3' },
];

function Product() {
    const { id } = useParams();
    const product = products.find(p => p.id === parseInt(id));
    if (!product) return <p>Product not found</p>;
  return (
      <div>
          <h1>{product.name}</h1>
          <p>{product.description}</p>
          <nav>
           <Link to={`/products/${id}/reviews`}>Reviews</Link>
          </nav>
          <Outlet />
      </div>
```

```
    );
}
function ProductReviews() {
    const { id } = useParams();
  return (
        <p>Product Reviews for {id}</p>
    );
}
function ProductList() {
  return (
        <div>
            <h1>Products</h1>
            <ul>
                {products.map(product => (
                    <li key={product.id}>
                        <Link
to={`/products/${product.id}`}>{product.name}</Link>
                    </li>
                ))}
            </ul>
        </div>
    );
}
function App() {
    return (
        <BrowserRouter>
            <nav>
                <ul>
                    <li><Link to="/">Home</Link></li>
                    <li><Link to="/products">Products</Link></li>
                </ul>
            </nav>
            <Routes>
                <Route path="/" element={<h1>Home Page</h1>} />
                <Route path="/products" element={<ProductList />}
/>
                <Route path="/products/:id" element={<Product />}>
                    <Route path="reviews" element={<ProductReviews
/>} />
                </Route>
            </Routes>
        </BrowserRouter>
    );
}
export default App;
```

Here's what's happening:

- We are using the useParams hook in both the Product and ProductReviews components.
- The Product component has a dynamic route, and the ProductReviews component is nested inside of the Product component using the <Outlet /> component.
- The ProductReviews will only be rendered when a user goes to the /products/:id/reviews page.
- We also display a link to /products/:id/reviews, when the product page is shown.

This example is now combining the functionality of dynamic routing and also nested routes.

Personal Insight

When I first started using React Router, I didn't know how useful dynamic and nested routes were. Now I use them to create complex layouts, and to display dynamic content. I really appreciate the flexibility of dynamic routes, and how it allows you to match multiple URLs with a single route.

Key Takeaways:

- Dynamic routes use parameters in the URL path, to access different data, using the useParams hook.
- Nested routes provide a hierarchical structure for organizing components, and the Outlet is used to display the nested routes.
- You can combine dynamic and nested routes to create much more complex applications.
- By using these patterns, you can create a truly flexible and dynamic experience for your end users.

With a good understanding of dynamic and nested routes, you can start building more advanced and organized React applications that handle complex scenarios with ease. This will also allow you to create more scalable code, as your application continues to grow.

6.3 PROTECTED ROUTES AND AUTHENTICATION: SECURING YOUR APPLICATION

In many applications, you'll need to have specific parts of the application that are only accessible to logged-in users. This is where protected routes come into play. Protected routes use authentication to verify that a user is logged in, and if the user is not logged in, they are redirected to a login page. This mechanism is essential for maintaining the security of your application.

Understanding Protected Routes

Protected routes are routes that can only be accessed by authenticated users. If a user attempts to access a protected route without being authenticated, they should be redirected to a login page. This ensures that unauthorized users don't have access to sensitive data.

Key concepts of protected routes:

- **Authentication**: Verification of a user's identity to grant them access to certain parts of the application.
- **Route Protection**: Wrapping components with a higher order component to ensure that a user is authorized.
- **Redirection**: Redirecting users to the login page when they try to access a protected route without being logged in.

Implementing Protected Routes

Let's implement an example where we're going to create a protected route that is only accessible by logged in users.

```
import React, { useState, createContext, useContext } from 'react';
import { BrowserRouter, Routes, Route, Link, useNavigate, Navigate } from 'react-router-dom';

const AuthContext = createContext(null);

function AuthProvider({ children }) {
  const [isLoggedIn, setIsLoggedIn] = useState(false);
  const login = () => setIsLoggedIn(true);
  const logout = () => setIsLoggedIn(false);
    return (
      <AuthContext.Provider value={{ isLoggedIn, login, logout }}>
        {children}
      </AuthContext.Provider>
    );
}
```

```
function useAuth() {
    return useContext(AuthContext);
}

function ProtectedRoute({ children }) {
    const { isLoggedIn } = useAuth();
    if (!isLoggedIn) {
        return <Navigate to="/login" />;
    }
    return children;
}
function Dashboard() {
    return <h1>Dashboard</h1>;
}

function Login() {
    const { login } = useAuth();
    const navigate = useNavigate();
    function handleLogin(){
        login();
        navigate("/dashboard")
    }
  return (
      <div>
          <h1>Login Page</h1>
        <button onClick={handleLogin}>Login</button>
      </div>
  );
}
function App() {
    return (
        <BrowserRouter>
            <AuthProvider>
              <nav>
                <ul>
                  <li><Link to="/">Home</Link></li>
                  <li><Link to="/dashboard">Dashboard</Link></li>
                </ul>
              </nav>
            <Routes>
              <Route path="/" element={<h1>Home Page</h1>} />
              <Route path="/login" element={<Login />} />
            <Route path="/dashboard" element={
              <ProtectedRoute>
                <Dashboard />
              </ProtectedRoute>
              }
            />
            </Routes>
            </AuthProvider>
        </BrowserRouter>
```

```
    );
}
export default App;
```

Let's explore the implementation:

1. **AuthContext and AuthProvider**: We are using the Context API to manage the state of our authentication.
   - We are creating our AuthContext using the createContext function, that we use to share the isLoggedIn state, and the login, and logout functions.
   - We are then creating our AuthProvider, which uses the useState hook to keep track of the current authentication status. The login function sets the isLoggedIn state to true, and the logout sets the isLoggedIn state to false.
   - Lastly, we are using the AuthContext.Provider to provide all of this state to the child components.
2. **useAuth Hook**: We create a custom hook useAuth, which allows us to consume our auth context from any of our components.
3. **ProtectedRoute Component**: The ProtectedRoute component is our higher order component that will ensure that users are authorized before they can view a route.
   - We use the useAuth hook to access the current authentication status using the isLoggedIn state.
   - If the user is not logged in, then we will redirect them to the login page using the Navigate component.
   - If the user is logged in, then we will render the children of the ProtectedRoute component, which is the protected component.
4. **Dashboard Component**: This is a simple component that can only be viewed when the user is logged in.
5. **Login Component**: The Login component is a simple page that allows users to log in. We are using the useAuth hook to trigger a state change when the user logs in, and the useNavigate hook to redirect the user to the dashboard page after a successful login.
6. **App Component:** Our App component wraps the routes in our AuthProvider, and also wraps the /dashboard route using the ProtectedRoute component, ensuring that our /dashboard page is protected.

By using the ProtectedRoute component, we can now easily protect any of our routes. This will ensure that only authorized users can access our protected components.

Practical Implementation: Accessing User Data

Let's expand on the previous example, where we are also going to store the user data when the user logs in.

```javascript
import React, { useState, createContext, useContext } from
'react';
import { BrowserRouter, Routes, Route, Link, useNavigate, Navigate
} from 'react-router-dom';

const AuthContext = createContext(null);

function AuthProvider({ children }) {
    const [user, setUser] = useState(null);

    const login = (userData) => {
      setUser(userData)
    }
    const logout = () => {
        setUser(null);
    }
    return (
        <AuthContext.Provider value={{ user, login, logout }}>
          {children}
        </AuthContext.Provider>
    );
}
function useAuth() {
    return useContext(AuthContext);
}
function ProtectedRoute({ children }) {
    const { user } = useAuth();
  if (!user) {
    return <Navigate to="/login" />;
  }
  return children;
}
function Dashboard() {
    const { user } = useAuth();
    return (
        <div>
          <h1>Dashboard</h1>
          <p>Welcome {user?.name}</p>
        </div>
    );
}
function Login() {
    const { login } = useAuth();
    const navigate = useNavigate();
    function handleLogin() {
```

```
        // Simulate a login and get user data
        const userData = { id: 1, name: 'John Doe' };
      login(userData);
        navigate("/dashboard");
    }
  return (
      <div>
        <h1>Login Page</h1>
        <button onClick={handleLogin}>Login</button>
      </div>
  );
}
function App() {
    return (
      <BrowserRouter>
        <AuthProvider>
          <nav>
            <ul>
              <li><Link to="/">Home</Link></li>
              <li><Link to="/dashboard">Dashboard</Link></li>
            </ul>
          </nav>
            <Routes>
              <Route path="/" element={<h1>Home Page</h1>} />
              <Route path="/login" element={<Login />} />
              <Route path="/dashboard" element={{
                <ProtectedRoute>
                    <Dashboard />
                </ProtectedRoute>
              }
            />
            </Routes>
        </AuthProvider>
      </BrowserRouter>
    );
}
export default App;
```

Here's how we've updated our code:

- **User Data:** Instead of only storing whether the user is logged in or not, we are now storing user information.
    - In our AuthProvider we are now storing the user object, which we are also updating in our login function.
- **Accessing User Data**: In our Dashboard component we are using our useAuth hook to access the user data, and then displaying it on the screen.

By storing user data when a user logs in, you can now provide a personalized user experience.

Personal Insight

I remember when I first had to implement authentication for a React application, I found it very difficult, and I had to rely on many different packages to achieve it. Now with React Router's Navigate component, and the Context API, it's much simpler to build a protected route. I find that combining these two concepts make authentication much easier to implement.

Key Takeaways:

- Protected routes are used to secure sensitive areas of your application.
- You can use the Navigate component from react-router-dom to redirect users if they are not authorized.
- You can use the Context API to store the user's state, and to manage the authentication status.
- You can create custom hooks to access the authentication context, and to simplify usage across multiple components.

By mastering protected routes, you'll be able to create applications with secure access to specific resources and provide a seamless user experience. This is essential for any application that requires authentication.

6.4 OPTIMIZING ROUTE PERFORMANCE: ENSURING SPEED AND RESPONSIVENESS

As your React application becomes more complex, you might find that your load times start to increase, which can result in a poor user experience. You want to ensure that your application is responsive and snappy. This is why performance optimization is so important, and you will need to utilize many different tools to do it.

Code Splitting: Reducing Initial Load Time

Code splitting is a technique that allows you to break down your application into smaller chunks that are loaded on demand. In traditional web applications, the entire JavaScript application was loaded when the user visits the page for the first time. With code splitting, you are loading different parts of the application when they are needed. This approach reduces the amount of JavaScript that needs to be downloaded initially, resulting in a much faster initial load time.

Lazy Loading: Loading Components on Demand

Lazy loading is a specific implementation of code splitting where components are only loaded when they are needed. This is extremely useful when you have many routes that you will be loading.

Let's see how you can implement lazy loading in React Router:

```jsx
import React, { Suspense, lazy } from 'react';
import { BrowserRouter, Routes, Route, Link } from 'react-router-dom';

const Home = lazy(() => import('./Home'));
const About = lazy(() => import('./About'));
const Contact = lazy(() => import('./Contact'));

function App() {
    return (
        <BrowserRouter>
            <nav>
              <ul>
                <li><Link to="/">Home</Link></li>
                <li><Link to="/about">About</Link></li>
                <li><Link to="/contact">Contact</Link></li>
              </ul>
            </nav>
            <Suspense fallback={<p>Loading...</p>}>
              <Routes>
                <Route path="/" element={<Home />} />
                <Route path="/about" element={<About />} />
                <Route path="/contact" element={<Contact />} />
              </Routes>
            </Suspense>
        </BrowserRouter>
    );
}
export default App;
```

Here's a breakdown of what we're doing:

1. **lazy Function**: The lazy function from React is used to load a component only when it needs to be rendered. It takes in a function that returns a promise containing a component.

129

2. **Suspense Component**: The Suspense component is used to display a fallback UI (in our case, a loading message) while the component is being loaded. We have wrapped our Routes component in Suspense so that it can display a loading message while the components are being loaded.
3. **Route Definitions**: When the user navigates to a route, then the lazy function will be used to fetch the component that we want to display.

With this implementation, our components will only be loaded when we navigate to their respective routes.

Memoization: Preventing Unnecessary Re-Renders

Memoization is a technique where we cache the results of expensive computations, and then return the cached value instead of performing the computation again. This is done if the inputs of the computation do not change, and helps to improve performance by avoiding unnecessary work. In React, memoization can be implemented using the useMemo and useCallback hooks.

Let's take a look at an example of how we can prevent re-renders using useCallback:

```
import React, { useState, useCallback } from 'react';
import { BrowserRouter, Routes, Route, Link } from 'react-router-dom';

function Home({ onButtonClick }) {
  console.log("Home component rendered")
    return (
        <div>
            <h1>Home</h1>
            <button onClick={onButtonClick}>Click</button>
        </div>
    );
}

function About() {
  console.log("About component rendered");
    return <h1>About</h1>
}
function App() {
  const [count, setCount] = useState(0);
    const handleClick = useCallback(() => {
        setCount(prevCount => prevCount + 1);
    }, [])
    return (
        <BrowserRouter>
            <nav>
                <ul>
```

130

```
            <li><Link to="/">Home</Link></li>
              <li><Link to="/about">About</Link></li>
            </ul>
          </nav>
          <Routes>
              <Route path="/" element={<Home
onButtonClick={handleClick} />} />
              <Route path="/about" element={<About />} />
          </Routes>
        <p>Count: {count}</p>
        </BrowserRouter>
    );
}
export default App;
```

Here's how we're using useCallback:

- We are passing a prop called onButtonClick to the Home component, that updates the state of the parent component.
- We are using the useCallback hook to cache the handleClick function, so that a new function is not being created when the parent component re-renders. Without using useCallback, the Home component will always re-render.
- We are also logging to the console to let you know when the components are rendered.

By using useCallback we ensure that the child component is only being re-rendered if it needs to, and also avoid re-creating functions on each render.

Practical Implementation: Lazy Loading and Memoization

Let's combine lazy loading and memoization into one example. We are going to use the React.memo component which will prevent re-renders of a component, unless its props have changed.

```
        import React, { useState, useCallback, Suspense, lazy, memo }
from 'react';
import { BrowserRouter, Routes, Route, Link } from 'react-router-
dom';

const Home = memo(function Home({ onButtonClick }) {
  console.log("Home component rendered");
    return (
        <div>
            <h1>Home</h1>
            <button onClick={onButtonClick}>Click</button>
```

```
        </div>
    );
});

const About = lazy(() => import('./About'));

function App() {
  const [count, setCount] = useState(0);
  const handleClick = useCallback(() => {
      setCount(prevCount => prevCount + 1);
  }, []);
    return (
        <BrowserRouter>
            <nav>
                <ul>
                  <li><Link to="/">Home</Link></li>
                  <li><Link to="/about">About</Link></li>
                </ul>
            </nav>
          <Suspense fallback={<p>Loading...</p>}>
            <Routes>
              <Route path="/" element={<Home
onButtonClick={handleClick} />} />
                <Route path="/about" element={<About />} />
              </Routes>
            </Suspense>
          <p>Count: {count}</p>
        </BrowserRouter>
    );
}
export default App;
```

Here's the breakdown:

- We are using lazy to load the About component.
- We are wrapping our Routes component in Suspense, to display a loading message while the component is loading.
- We are also using the memo function to wrap our Home component, to prevent it from re-rendering if the props do not change.
- Lastly we are using useCallback to cache our handleClick function.

With this implementation, the Home component will no longer re-render when the parent component re-renders, and the About component will only be loaded when the /about route is navigated to.

Personal Insight

As a React developer, I've learned that performance optimization is crucial, especially for larger applications. When I first started, I didn't realize the importance of using tools such as code splitting, lazy loading and memoization. Now these are tools that I am consciously using in each of my applications to make sure the users get the best experience. I often find myself using React's profiler to find the slow parts of my application, and then using techniques such as these to fix the slow parts of the code.

Key Takeaways:

- Code splitting helps you reduce the initial load time by splitting up your application into smaller chunks.
- Lazy loading is a technique used to load components on demand, which makes it a great tool for code splitting.
- Memoization can be used to prevent unnecessary re-renders by caching the result of expensive operations.
- Using the combination of code splitting, lazy loading, and memoization, you can create an application that is both fast, and performs well for your end users.

By understanding these optimization techniques, you'll be able to ensure that your React applications are performant and scalable, even as they grow in size and complexity. This is an essential skill to learn when building any modern React application.

CHAPTER 7: FORMS AND USER INPUT HANDLING

Forms are a fundamental part of web applications. They are how you collect data from your users. This chapter will guide you through the various ways you can handle forms and user input in React, including the differences between controlled and uncontrolled components, advanced form management libraries, validation, and file uploads.

Okay, let's delve into the fundamental concepts of controlled and uncontrolled components in React, focusing on how they handle form inputs. Understanding the differences between these two approaches is crucial for building robust and maintainable forms. We'll explore their characteristics, use cases, and practical implementations.

7.1 CONTROLLED VS. UNCONTROLLED COMPONENTS: MANAGING FORM DATA IN REACT

When you're dealing with form elements in React, you have a choice in how you manage the data that users input: controlled or uncontrolled components. These two approaches represent different ways of handling form values, and understanding them is essential for building dynamic forms.

Controlled Components: React is in Control

In controlled components, the form's data is entirely managed by React. The input element's value is tied to the state, and any changes in the input trigger a state update. Think of it as React being the single source of truth.

Let's take a look at a practical example:

```
import React, { useState } from 'react';
function ControlledInput(){
   const [inputValue, setInputValue] = useState('');
  function handleChange(event){
    setInputValue(event.target.value)
  }
   return (
```

```
        <input
            type="text"
            value={inputValue}
            onChange={handleChange}
        />
    );
}
export default ControlledInput;
```

Here's a step-by-step explanation:

1. **State Initialization:** We use the useState hook to initialize the inputValue with an empty string. This will hold the current value of the text field.
2. **value Prop:** We are passing in the inputValue state as the value prop to the input element. This tells React that this is a controlled component, and React should be in charge of the value of this component.
3. **onChange Event Handler**: We are creating a function to handle any changes that happen to the input field.
4. **Updating State**: Whenever the input's value changes, the handleChange function is triggered, which calls setInputValue to update the state with the latest value entered by the user. This re-renders the component and updates the input field.

This code establishes a connection between the input's value and the React state, ensuring that React is always in control of what the user sees in the text field.

Benefits of Controlled Components

- **Fine-Grained Control:** Because React is in control, you have precise control over every aspect of the input, from the value that is displayed, to whether you will allow a user to type in a value.
- **Validation:** Validation is easier to implement, because you can add validation functions in the onChange handler, so that the state is not updated unless the input is valid.
- **Live Updates**: You can implement live updates of the input's values, giving you much more flexibility.
- **Conditional Rendering:** You can dynamically update the input based on the state of the application.

Uncontrolled Components: Letting the DOM Handle Data

In contrast, uncontrolled components store the input's value within the DOM. React does not directly control the input's value. Instead, you'll use a React ref to get data directly from the DOM when necessary (e.g. form submission). React has no way of knowing that the value of the input has changed, unless the component is re-rendered for some other reason.

Here's a basic example of an uncontrolled input:

```
import React, { useRef } from 'react';
function UncontrolledInput() {
    const inputRef = useRef(null);
  function handleSubmit(e){
        e.preventDefault();
        console.log(inputRef.current.value)
    }
  return (
        <form onSubmit={handleSubmit}>
          <input type="text" ref={inputRef} />
            <button type="submit">Submit</button>
        </form>
    );
}
export default UncontrolledInput;
```

Let's go through it step by step:

1. **useRef Hook:** We use the useRef hook to create a reference to our input element using the variable inputRef.
2. **ref Prop:** The ref prop is set to inputRef, which connects it to the input element, allowing us to get direct access to that DOM element.
3. **handleSubmit Function:** When the form is submitted, we prevent the default behavior of refreshing the page, and then we use inputRef.current.value to access the current value of the input element in the DOM.

Benefits of Uncontrolled Components:

- **Simpler Setup:** Requires less code, which makes it ideal for very basic forms, where you do not need the benefits of controlled components.
- **Easier Integration with Third-Party Libraries**: Can be easier to implement with third-party libraries.

Practical Implementation: Comparing Controlled and Uncontrolled Components

Let's create a component that uses a controlled input and another that uses an uncontrolled input, so that you can see the different behavior of the two components.

```
import React, { useState, useRef } from 'react';

function FormExample() {
    const [controlledValue, setControlledValue] = useState('');
    const inputRef = useRef(null);

    function handleControlledChange(e) {
        setControlledValue(e.target.value);
    }
   function handleUncontrolledSubmit(e) {
        e.preventDefault();
        console.log(`Uncontrolled Value:
${inputRef.current.value}`);
    }
    return (
        <div>
            <h2>Controlled Component:</h2>
            <input
              type="text"
              value={controlledValue}
              onChange={handleControlledChange}
            />
            <p>Controlled Value: {controlledValue}</p>
            <h2>Uncontrolled Component:</h2>
            <form onSubmit={handleUncontrolledSubmit}>
                <input type="text" ref={inputRef} />
                <button type="submit">Submit</button>
            </form>
        </div>
    );
}
export default FormExample;
```

Here's a breakdown:

- We create two input fields: one controlled and one uncontrolled.
- In the controlled input, we manage the value using the state and update it on every change.
- In the uncontrolled input, we use a ref to get the value of the input only when the form is submitted.

With this implementation, you will see that the controlled input will update with every change, and that the uncontrolled input will only show a value when the form is submitted.

Personal Insight

I remember when I first started learning React, I didn't really understand the difference between controlled and uncontrolled components. I tried to implement my forms with uncontrolled components, and realized very quickly how limiting they were. After I learned how to use controlled components, I found that my application became much more dynamic, and I was able to easily implement validation and live updates. Now I default to controlled components for all my forms.

Key Takeaways:

- Controlled components manage the input value using React state, giving you full control of the input's value.
- Uncontrolled components manage the input values by relying on the DOM, and are easier to implement for very simple forms.
- Controlled components are much more flexible, and they are much easier to validate.
- Uncontrolled components are good for very simple forms where you don't need granular control of the values.
- As a general rule, you should use controlled components whenever possible.

By understanding the differences between controlled and uncontrolled components, you'll be able to make the right choices when developing React applications that use forms. This will result in better designed, and more scalable applications.

7.2 MANAGING FORMS WITH REACT HOOK FORM: SIMPLIFYING FORM LOGIC

While controlled components provide a good base for handling forms, they can quickly become difficult to manage as forms get more complex. This is where libraries like React Hook Form shine. React Hook Form is a library that takes a different approach, where it focuses on performance and scalability, using uncontrolled components under the hood, while still giving you the flexibility that comes with using controlled components. It minimizes re-renders, simplifies validation, and handles form state efficiently.

Key Features of React Hook Form

- **Performance:** React Hook Form is very performant as it reduces the amount of re-renders, by managing all the state internally, without having to re-render the components.
- **Uncontrolled Components**: Uses uncontrolled components under the hood, which prevents re-renders that are not needed.
- **Ease of Use:** Provides a simple and intuitive API, simplifying complex form logic.
- **Validation**: Handles client-side validation efficiently and intuitively.
- **Flexibility:** Allows for complex form scenarios, such as dynamic forms, multi-step forms, and nested forms.

Setting Up React Hook Form

To use React Hook Form, you will first need to install it:

```
npm install react-hook-form
```

Basic Form Implementation with React Hook Form

Let's start with the basic implementation of React Hook Form, where we're going to create a simple form with a name and email input.

```jsx
import React from 'react';
import { useForm } from 'react-hook-form';
function BasicForm() {
   const { register, handleSubmit, formState: { errors } } =
useForm();
  function onSubmit(data) {
    console.log(data);
  }
    return (
        <form onSubmit={handleSubmit(onSubmit)}>
          <label>
            Name:
            <input type="text" {...register("name")} />
          </label>
          {errors.name && <p>Name is required</p>}
          <label>
            Email:
            <input type="email" {...register("email")} />
          </label>
            {errors.email && <p>Email is required</p>}
            <button type="submit">Submit</button>
        </form>
    );
```

```
}
export default BasicForm;
```

Let's walk through the code:

1. **useForm Hook:** We are importing the useForm hook from the react-hook-form library.
2. **Destructuring useForm:** We are destructuring the useForm hook, which returns three very useful values:
   - o register: A function that registers an input field and also allows you to use validation, and more functionality. This function will return all the props that you need to pass into your inputs.
   - o handleSubmit: A function that handles the form submission, and also validates the fields, before calling the function that is passed to it as a prop.
   - o formState: This object contains all the useful information about the form, including a list of all the errors if any of the validations have failed.
3. **Registering Input Fields**: We register the input fields using the register function, and we also pass in the name property of the input as a key. The register function will then return all the props that you will need to use in your input field, including the value, and onChange functions.
4. **handleSubmit function**: We are passing the handleSubmit function to our onSubmit prop. This will prevent the default behavior of submitting the form, validate the input fields, and call the onSubmit function, with the form's data.
5. **Displaying Errors**: If there is an error, we are going to conditionally render an error message.

Form Validation with React Hook Form

React Hook Form provides a simple way of handling validations using the register function. In the previous example we did not add any specific validation rules to our fields, but we will now.

```
    import React from 'react';
import { useForm } from 'react-hook-form';
function ValidationForm() {
  const { register, handleSubmit, formState: { errors } } =
useForm();
   function onSubmit(data) {
       console.log(data);
```

```
    }
    return (
      <form onSubmit={handleSubmit(onSubmit)}>
        <label>
          Name:
          <input type="text" {...register("name", { required:
"Name is required!" })} />
        </label>
          {errors.name && <p>{errors.name.message}</p>}
        <label>
          Email:
          <input type="email" {...register("email", {
            required: "Email is required!",
          pattern: {
              value: /^[A-Z0-9._%+-]+@[A-Z0-9.-]+\.[A-
Z]{2,}$/i,
              message: "Invalid email address",
            },
          })} />
        </label>
          {errors.email && <p>{errors.email.message}</p>}
        <button type="submit">Submit</button>
      </form>
  );
}
export default ValidationForm;
```

Let's go through the new parts:

1. **Validation Rules:** We are passing in a second argument to our register
   function, which is an object, containing all our validation rules.
   o   For the name field, we are using required to indicate that this field is
       required, and also passing in an error message that is displayed to the
       user.
   o   For the email field, we are using required to make the field required,
       and then using pattern to create a regular expression that will ensure
       the value is in the correct email format. We are also passing in an
       error message.

Practical Implementation: Dynamic Forms

Let's expand on our previous examples and create a dynamic form where users can
add new input fields:

```
    import React from 'react';
import { useForm, useFieldArray } from 'react-hook-form';
```

```
function DynamicForm() {
    const { register, handleSubmit, control, formState: { errors }
} = useForm({
        defaultValues: {
            skills: [{ name: '' }],
        },
    });
    const { fields, append, remove } = useFieldArray({
        control,
        name: 'skills',
    });
  function onSubmit(data) {
    console.log(data);
  }
  return (
    <form onSubmit={handleSubmit(onSubmit)}>
      <ul>
        {fields.map((field, index) => (
          <li key={field.id}>
            <label>
              Skill:
              <input type="text"
{...register(`skills.${index}.name`, { required: "Skill is
required" })} />
              {errors.skills?.[index]?.name && (
                <p>{errors.skills?.[index]?.name?.message}</p>
              )}
            </label>
            <button type="button" onClick={() =>
remove(index)}>Remove</button>
          </li>
        ))}
      </ul>
        <button type="button" onClick={() => append({ name: ''
})}>Add Skill</button>
        <button type="submit">Submit</button>
    </form>
  );
}
export default DynamicForm;
```

Here's how this example works:

1. **useFieldArray Hook**: We are using the useFieldArray hook to manage an array of form fields.
2. **fields Array:** This is an array that represents the current list of skill fields. This contains a list of unique ids for each field.

3. **append function:** This function is called to add a new entry to the skills array.
4. **remove function:** This function is called to remove an entry from the skills array.
5. **Dynamic Input fields:** We are creating dynamic input fields using the fields array, and the register function.
6. **Validation:** We are also passing in the required prop to our register function to validate our fields.

Using React Hook Form makes dynamic forms like this a much more easier to implement.

Personal Insight

When I first started using React, I found form handling to be one of the most tedious aspects of development. Managing all of the state and updating input values on each event felt very verbose. Once I started using React Hook Form, I found that my forms were much more streamlined, and the amount of boilerplate was significantly reduced. I also really like how React Hook Form is optimized for performance, and only re-renders when necessary.

Key Takeaways:

- React Hook Form is a powerful library for managing forms in React applications that provides an easy to use API.
- It uses uncontrolled components under the hood, which prevents re-renders.
- It provides a simple way to implement client side validation.
- It is very performant, and does not re-render unnecessarily.
- It can easily handle complex form scenarios, such as dynamic forms.

By using React Hook Form, you can build complex forms with ease and confidence. This library is a game changer and a must have tool in your toolkit.

7.3 VALIDATION WITH YUP AND ZOD: ENSURING DATA INTEGRITY

Form validation is a crucial step in the development process of web applications. Without validation, you may run into issues with unexpected input formats, which could cause errors in the application. You need a way to ensure that your users provide the correct and expected data, and that data is in a valid format before sending to your backend. Yup and Zod are two popular libraries that provide schema based validation, and makes the process of validation very efficient.

Yup: Schema-Based Validation

Yup is a JavaScript schema builder for value parsing and validation. It allows you to create schemas that define the structure and validation rules for your data. It's often used to validate form data, but can also be used to validate data from any source.

To use Yup, you need to first install it: npm install yup

Let's start with a practical example of how you can implement Yup in a React application using React Hook Form:

```javascript
import React from 'react';
import { useForm } from 'react-hook-form';
import { yupResolver } from '@hookform/resolvers/yup';
import * as yup from 'yup';

const schema = yup.object({
    name: yup.string().required("Name is required"),
    email: yup.string().email("Invalid email
format").required("Email is required"),
});
function YupForm() {
    const { register, handleSubmit, formState: { errors } } =
useForm({
        resolver: yupResolver(schema)
    });

  function onSubmit(data){
      console.log(data);
    }
    return (
      <form onSubmit={handleSubmit(onSubmit)}>
        <label>
          Name:
          <input type="text" {...register("name")} />
        </label>
        {errors.name && <p>{errors.name?.message}</p>}
          <label>
          Email:
            <input type="email" {...register("email")} />
          </label>
          {errors.email && <p>{errors.email?.message}</p>}
        <button type="submit">Submit</button>
      </form>
    );
```

```
}
export default YupForm;
```

Here's a breakdown of what's happening:

1. **Schema Definition:** First, we're creating our validation schema using Yup, with the yup.object function.
   - **name**: We are validating our name field, ensuring that it is a string and that it is required. We are passing in a custom error message to the .required function, which is what will be displayed to the user when the validation fails.
   - **email**: We are validating our email field, ensuring that it is a string, it is in a valid email format, and is also required. We are also passing in custom error messages to the .email, and .required functions, which will be displayed to the user.
2. **yupResolver:** We use the yupResolver from @hookform/resolvers/yup, and pass in the schema that we just created. This function will validate the form fields based on the Yup schema.
3. **register Function:** We are using the register function, from the useForm hook, to register our input fields.
4. **Error Handling:** If the form is invalid, we can access the errors from the formState object, which will contain an errors object, that contains all of our errors. We are displaying the error messages for our fields if there are any.

Zod: TypeScript-First Schema Validation

Zod is another popular validation library that provides a TypeScript-first approach to schema declaration and validation. It focuses on typesafety, and uses a very similar api as Yup.

Let's implement the same example using Zod:

First install it using: npm install zod

```
import React from 'react';
import { useForm } from 'react-hook-form';
import { zodResolver } from '@hookform/resolvers/zod';
import { z } from 'zod';

const schema = z.object({
  name: z.string().min(1, { message: "Name is required" }),
   email: z.string().email({ message: "Invalid email format"
}).min(1, { message: "Email is required" }),
```

```
});
function ZodForm() {
    const { register, handleSubmit, formState: { errors } } =
useForm({
        resolver: zodResolver(schema),
    });
    function onSubmit(data){
      console.log(data);
    }
    return (
      <form onSubmit={handleSubmit(onSubmit)}>
        <label>
          Name:
          <input type="text" {...register("name")} />
        </label>
          {errors.name && <p>{errors.name.message}</p>}
        <label>
          Email:
          <input type="email" {...register("email")} />
        </label>
          {errors.email && <p>{errors.email.message}</p>}
        <button type="submit">Submit</button>
      </form>
    );
}
export default ZodForm;
```

Here's a breakdown of what's happening:

1. **Schema Definition**: The schema definition is similar to Yup, but the way that we validate is slightly different.
   o We are using z.object to define an object, that contains the validation rules.
   o **name**: We are using z.string() to say that it has to be a string, and that it needs to have a minimum length of 1. We are also defining a custom error message that is displayed when this rule is violated.
   o **email**: We are using z.string() and .email() to define that it should be a string in a valid email format, as well as having a minimum length of one character. We are also defining a custom error message for each validation rule.
2. **zodResolver**: We are using the zodResolver from @hookform/resolvers/zod to integrate our validation schema with React Hook Form.
3. **register Function:** We are using the register function from useForm to connect our input fields with React Hook Form.

4. **Error Handling**: If the form is invalid, we can access the error messages from the errors object.

Practical Implementation: Validating an Object

Let's expand on our previous examples and validate an object of data, to see how these libraries work in more complex scenarios.

First, let's validate the object with Yup:

```
      import React from 'react';
import { useForm } from 'react-hook-form';
import { yupResolver } from '@hookform/resolvers/yup';
import * as yup from 'yup';
const schema = yup.object({
  userData: yup.object({
    name: yup.string().required("Name is required"),
    email: yup.string().email("Invalid email
format").required("Email is required"),
  })
});

function YupObjectForm() {
  const { register, handleSubmit, formState: { errors } } =
useForm({
      resolver: yupResolver(schema)
  });
    function onSubmit(data) {
        console.log(data);
    }
    return (
      <form onSubmit={handleSubmit(onSubmit)}>
         .<label>
            Name:
           <input type="text" {...register("userData.name")} />
         </label>
            {errors.userData?.name &&
<p>{errors.userData.name?.message}</p>}
         <label>
            Email:
           <input type="email" {...register("userData.email")} />
        </label>
           {errors.userData?.email &&
<p>{errors.userData.email?.message}</p>}
       <button type="submit">Submit</button>
    </form>
    );
}
export default YupObjectForm;
```

content_copy download
Use code **with caution**.Jsx
And let's do the same example with Zod:

```jsx
import React from 'react';
import { useForm } from 'react-hook-form';
import { zodResolver } from '@hookform/resolvers/zod';
import { z } from 'zod';

const schema = z.object({
    userData: z.object({
        name: z.string().min(1, { message: "Name is required" }),
        email: z.string().email({ message: "Invalid email format" }).min(1, { message: "Email is required" }),
    })
});
function ZodObjectForm() {
  const { register, handleSubmit, formState: { errors } } = useForm({
    resolver: zodResolver(schema),
  });

  function onSubmit(data) {
      console.log(data);
  }
  return (
    <form onSubmit={handleSubmit(onSubmit)}>
        <label>
          Name:
          <input type="text" {...register("userData.name")} />
        </label>
        {errors.userData?.name &&
<p>{errors.userData.name?.message}</p>}
        <label>
          Email:
            <input type="email" {...register("userData.email")} />
        </label>
        {errors.userData?.email &&
<p>{errors.userData.email?.message}</p>}
        <button type="submit">Submit</button>
    </form>
    );
}
export default ZodObjectForm;
```

Here's what we're doing:

- **Schema**: We are validating an object called userData using both Yup and Zod.
- **Validation:** Both Yup and Zod offer very similar ways to validate objects.
- **Registering fields**: We are registering the input fields using dot notation to access the correct field.
- **Error Handling:** If there are any errors, then it is displayed in the errors object, as well as nested in the correct field object.

With both Yup and Zod, you have a very flexible and powerful way of defining how data is structured and validated. This makes building forms in React much easier.

Personal Insight

When I started building complex forms in React, I realized that the built-in validation methods were just not enough. I had to write complex code to validate each of my fields. I was very happy when I discovered Yup, because the schema based approach to validation is something that I always wished existed. After that I discovered Zod, which is also fantastic for schema based validation. I often use them to create schemas that I can share between my client and server code.

Key Takeaways:

- Yup is a schema builder for value parsing and validation, it is a great tool to validate data in forms.
- Zod is a TypeScript-first schema declaration and validation library that is very similar to Yup, with better type safety.
- Both libraries provide a very robust and flexible way of validating data in forms.
- You can easily integrate these libraries with React Hook Form using resolvers.

By understanding how to use Yup and Zod, you will be able to create highly robust and dynamic forms in React, while ensuring that all of your data is validated. This is an essential skill for any front-end developer.

7.4 HANDLING FILE UPLOADS AND DRAG & DROP: ENRICHING USER INTERACTIONS

File uploads and drag-and-drop capabilities can significantly enhance user interactions, allowing users to upload documents, images, and other media.

Implementing these features can often be a daunting task, but React combined with modern HTML APIs can make this process much simpler. Let's explore how to implement these in React.

Implementing Basic File Uploads

The simplest way to implement file uploads is using the HTML input element with type="file". Let's create a basic component that will display a file input:

```
import React, { useRef } from 'react';

function FileUpload() {
    const fileInputRef = useRef(null);

    function handleSubmit(event) {
        event.preventDefault();
        if (fileInputRef.current.files.length === 0) {
            console.log("No files selected.");
            return;
        }
    const file = fileInputRef.current.files[0];
     console.log("File: ", file)
        // Here is where you would send your file to the server
    }
    return (
      <form onSubmit={handleSubmit}>
        <input type="file" ref={fileInputRef} />
        <button type="submit">Upload File</button>
      </form>
    );
}
export default FileUpload;
```

Here's what's happening:

1. **useRef Hook**: We are creating a ref using the useRef hook, which will be connected to our input field, to directly access its DOM element.
2. **input type="file"**: We're creating an HTML input element with the type "file", and also passing in the ref.
3. **handleSubmit Function**: When the form is submitted, we prevent the default behavior of refreshing the page using event.preventDefault(), and then check if the user selected any files by looking at the fileInputRef.current.files property. If no files have been selected we return early.

4. **File Access**: The files that are selected by the user are stored in an array called files in our input element. We access the first file in the array using the index [0], which we will then log to the console, but you can do anything you want with the file at this point, such as uploading it to your server using an API.

Multiple File Uploads

You can also allow multiple files to be uploaded by adding the multiple attribute to the input element:

```
import React, { useRef } from 'react';
function MultipleFileUpload() {
  const fileInputRef = useRef(null);

  function handleSubmit(event) {
      event.preventDefault();
      if (fileInputRef.current.files.length === 0) {
          console.log("No files selected.");
          return;
      }
  const files = Array.from(fileInputRef.current.files);
      console.log("Files: ", files)
    // Here is where you would send your file to the server
  }
  return (
      <form onSubmit={handleSubmit}>
          <input type="file" ref={fileInputRef} multiple />
          <button type="submit">Upload Files</button>
      </form>
  );
}
export default MultipleFileUpload;
```

Here's the difference in our implementation:

- We have added the multiple prop to the input element, allowing users to select multiple files.
- We are now converting the HTMLCollection of files to an array using Array.from(), so that we can use array methods on the files variable.

Implementing Drag & Drop File Uploads

Drag and drop functionality allows users to upload files by dragging them directly into the browser window.

151

Let's see how you can implement it:

```
import React, { useState } from 'react';

function DragDropUpload() {
    const [files, setFiles] = useState([]);
    function handleDragOver(event) {
        event.preventDefault();
    }
    function handleDrop(event) {
        event.preventDefault();
        const droppedFiles = Array.from(event.dataTransfer.files);
        setFiles(prevFiles => [...prevFiles, ...droppedFiles])
    }
    return (
        <div
            onDragOver={handleDragOver}
            onDrop={handleDrop}
            style={{
                border: '2px dashed #ccc',
                padding: '20px',
                textAlign: 'center'
            }}>
            <p>Drag & Drop Files Here!</p>
            <ul>
                {files.map(file => (
                    <li key={file.name}>{file.name}</li>
                ))}
            </ul>
        </div>
    );
}
export default DragDropUpload;
```

Here's a step-by-step explanation:

1. **files State**: We create a files state to keep track of all the files that have been dropped.
2. **onDragOver Event Handler**: The handleDragOver event handler prevents the browser from opening the file in a new tab, by preventing the default browser behavior.
3. **onDrop Event Handler**: This is triggered when the files are dropped. We are getting access to the files from event.dataTransfer.files, and then adding it to our state. We are converting the HTMLCollection to an array using Array.from, before storing the new list of files in the state.
4. **Displaying Files**: We are mapping over our files array, and displaying the name of each file.

Practical Implementation: Combining File Upload and Drag & Drop

Let's combine file upload with drag and drop, to create a more user friendly experience.

```
import React, { useState } from 'react';
function CombinedUpload() {
    const [files, setFiles] = useState([]);

  function handleDragOver(e) {
      e.preventDefault();
  }
  function handleDrop(e) {
    e.preventDefault();
      const droppedFiles = Array.from(e.dataTransfer.files);
        setFiles(prevFiles => [...prevFiles, ...droppedFiles]);
  }
  function handleFileChange(event) {
    const newFiles = Array.from(event.target.files);
    setFiles(prevFiles => [...prevFiles, ...newFiles])
  }
    return (
        <div>
            <div
              onDragOver={handleDragOver}
              onDrop={handleDrop}
              style={{
                border: '2px dashed #ccc',
                 padding: '20px',
                textAlign: 'center'
              }}>
            <p>Drag & Drop Files Here!</p>
          <input type="file" multiple onChange={handleFileChange}
/>
            <ul>
                {files.map(file => (
                  <li key={file.name}>{file.name}</li>
                ))}
            </ul>
        </div>
    </div>
    );
}
export default CombinedUpload;
```

Here's how the code is implemented:

- We are combining our previous implementations, by using the same HTML, but only handling different events.
- When the user drops files, the handleDrop function will be called, and if the user uses the input, the handleFileChange will be called.
- Both of those event handlers update the files state, and then display the files in the <ul> element.

This implementation will allow users to upload files using both drag and drop, as well as the traditional input method.

Personal Insight

I remember how intimidating it was when I first had to deal with file uploads. I had to learn a lot about the different javascript APIs, to make sure that my code could handle all of the edge cases. It's much easier now, but it's still very important to properly handle file uploads, so that you don't run into any issues. I find that combining file uploads and drag and drop gives a really nice user experience.

Key Takeaways:

- You can implement basic file uploads using the input element with the type "file".
- You can use the multiple attribute to allow users to upload multiple files.
- You can implement drag and drop by adding event handlers to a div element, and then retrieving the files from the event object.
- You can combine both methods to create a more flexible and intuitive user experience.

By understanding how to handle file uploads and implement drag-and-drop functionality, you'll be able to create web applications that can interact with files in a seamless and intuitive manner. These are essential features for building rich and dynamic user experiences.

CHAPTER 8: PERFORMANCE OPTIMIZATION IN REACT 19

Performance optimization is a critical skill for any React developer. As your applications grow in complexity, you need to be aware of the techniques that you can use to ensure your application is performant, and is responsive to user interactions. This chapter will guide you through all the different techniques for improving your React applications.

8.1 UNDERSTANDING REACT RENDERING BEHAVIOR: THE HEART OF PERFORMANCE OPTIMIZATION

React's rendering behavior determines how efficiently your application updates the UI in response to changes. React uses a virtual DOM to efficiently manage the updates, but knowing when and why a component re-renders is fundamental for performance optimization. A thorough understanding of React's rendering behavior is the first step towards optimizing any React application.

Key Principles of React Rendering

- **Initial Render**: When a component is first mounted, React creates a virtual DOM representation of the UI and then renders the output to the browser's DOM. This is the initial render, when a component is first created.
- **State Updates**: Whenever a component's state changes, using the useState hook, React will re-render the component. This means that if you update the state, the component will be re-rendered.
- **Prop Updates**: When a parent component renders, any child components that receive new props from that parent will also be re-rendered. This is important to know, because you may be passing down props to child components that don't need to re-render.
- **Context Updates**: If a component uses the Context API, then any changes in the context's value will cause that component, as well as its children, to re-render.
- **Reconciliation**: After a component is re-rendered, React's reconciliation algorithm will compare the previous virtual DOM with the new virtual DOM, and then determine the minimal number of changes that need to be

applied to the real DOM. This process is very performant, because React does not always re-render the entire DOM, only the parts that changed.

- **Default Behavior:** React will re-render components aggressively by default, which is why it is important to use optimization techniques, to prevent unnecessary re-renders.

How React's Virtual DOM Works

React's virtual DOM is a lightweight in-memory representation of the actual DOM. Instead of directly manipulating the actual DOM, React manipulates the virtual DOM, and then only updates the changed parts in the real DOM.

Here's a simplified view of how it works:

1. **Virtual DOM Creation:** React creates a new virtual DOM when state or props change, reflecting the new UI.
2. **Reconciliation Process:** React compares this new Virtual DOM with the previous virtual DOM using a "diffing" algorithm.
3. **Real DOM Update:** React applies only the minimal necessary changes to the actual DOM, making this a very performant process.

This process is designed to be as efficient as possible, and makes React apps feel responsive.

Identifying Unnecessary Re-renders

Before you can optimize your application's performance, you need to identify the parts of the application that are rendering too often. There are a few techniques that you can use to do this:

1. **Console Logging:** You can use console.log messages to identify when a component is re-rendering, and also look at the state and props, to see why it is re-rendering.
2. **React DevTools Profiler:** The React DevTools Profiler is the most powerful tool for identifying bottlenecks in your application. This will allow you to profile your application, see which components are slow to render, and find the exact reason for the re-render.

Let's start with console.log messages, and then we can look at the profiler.

```
import React, { useState } from 'react';
function MyComponent({ name }) {
```

```
  console.log(`MyComponent rendered with name: ${name}`);
    return (
      <p>Hello, {name}!</p>
    );
}
function App(){
    const [count, setCount] = useState(0);
    return (
      <div>
          <p>Count: {count}</p>
          <button onClick={() => setCount(prevCount => prevCount +
1)}>Increment</button>
        <MyComponent name="World" />
      </div>
    );
}
export default App;
```

Here's what's happening:

- We have a MyComponent component, and an App component.
- When we click the button, we update the count state, which causes the App component to re-render.
- We are logging a message to the console every time the MyComponent is rendered, as well as the current value of its prop name.

If you run this code, you can see that the MyComponent component is re-rendered every time that we click the button, even though its props are not changing. In more complex applications, this could lead to performance bottlenecks.

Using the React DevTools Profiler

The React DevTools Profiler is a much more powerful tool that allows you to see how long each component takes to render, and also find the exact reason for each re-render.

Here is how you use the profiler:

1. Open the React DevTools by pressing F12 in your browser, and then select the "Profiler" tab.
2. Click the record button, and then interact with your application.
3. Click stop recording.
4. You can now see how many times each component was rendered, as well as how long each component took to render.

Practical Implementation: Identifying and Fixing Re-renders

Let's take a look at a more practical example of identifying and fixing re-renders.

```
import React, { useState } from 'react';
function ChildComponent({ onClick }) {
    console.log("Child component rendered.");
  return (
    <button onClick={onClick}>Click</button>
  );
}
function ParentComponent(){
   const [count, setCount] = useState(0);
   function handleClick(){
       setCount(prevCount => prevCount + 1);
   }
   return (
       <div>
          <p>Count: {count}</p>
           <ChildComponent onClick={handleClick} />
       </div>
   );
}
export default ParentComponent;
```

Here is what is happening:

- We have a ChildComponent which has a button, and then a ParentComponent that has state, and calls the ChildComponent.
- Every time the button in the ParentComponent is clicked, then the ParentComponent is re-rendered, which will then cause the ChildComponent to re-render, even though the props to the ChildComponent did not change.

Using the Profiler, you can confirm that the ChildComponent re-renders unnecessarily. In the next section, we will use memoization to prevent unnecessary re-renders like this.

Personal Insight

When I first started using React, I often treated it as a magical library that just worked. I didn't really pay attention to React's rendering behavior, until I started building more complex applications, and realized that my applications were not as performant as I expected. This is why it is extremely important to have an understanding of how react re-renders components. Once I understood this behavior,

I found that it was much easier for me to optimize my code and identify where I had performance bottlenecks.

Key Takeaways:

- React re-renders components when state changes, prop changes, or context changes.
- The virtual DOM compares the old and new UI and only updates the changes in the real DOM.
- You can use console.log messages to see when a component is being rendered.
- The React DevTools Profiler is the best tool for finding the slow parts of your application, as well as the reasons for the re-renders.
- By understanding the React rendering behavior, you can write more performant code, and identify places where you need to use optimization techniques.

With a clear understanding of React rendering behavior, you'll be better equipped to diagnose performance issues and apply the right optimization strategies. This is the first, and most important step to optimizing any React application.

8.2 MEMOIZATION WITH USEMEMO AND USECALLBACK: CACHING FOR PERFORMANCE

Memoization is a technique where we cache the results of expensive function calls and reuse them if the inputs haven't changed. In React, this can significantly improve performance by preventing unnecessary computations and re-renders. React provides two powerful hooks: useMemo and useCallback that help you implement memoization in your components.

useMemo: Memoizing Values

The useMemo hook is used to memoize the result of an expensive calculation. It takes a function that performs the calculation and a dependency array. React will only re-execute the function if one of the dependencies has changed. Otherwise, it will return a cached value.

Here's the basic syntax:

```
import React, { useMemo } from 'react';
```

```
function MyComponent({ data }) {
  const memoizedValue = useMemo(() => {
    // Expensive calculation here
    return computedValue;
  }, [dependencies]);
  // Use the memoizedValue
}
```

Here's a breakdown of what's happening:

- useMemo(callback, [dependencies]): The useMemo hook takes two arguments:
  - callback: A function that performs an expensive computation, and returns the computed value.
  - [dependencies]: An array of dependencies. React will only re-execute the callback function if one of these dependencies has changed. If no dependencies are provided, then the function will only run once on mount.
- memoizedValue: The result of the computation, which is stored in the cache, and can be used later, if the dependencies haven't changed.

Practical Implementation: Expensive Computation

Let's take a look at a practical example of using useMemo to prevent an expensive calculation from running on every re-render:

```
import React, { useState, useMemo } from 'react';

function MyComponent({ data }) {
  const [count, setCount] = useState(0);
  const expensiveValue = useMemo(() => {
    console.log("Expensive operation called")
    let sum = 0;
    for (let i = 0; i < 100000000; i++) {
      sum += data + i;
    }
    return sum;
  }, [data]);
  function handleClick(){
    setCount(prevCount => prevCount + 1);
  }
  return (
    <div>
      <p>Count: {count}</p>
      <button onClick={handleClick}>Increment</button>
      <p>Expensive Value: {expensiveValue}</p>
```

```
        </div>
    );
}
export default MyComponent;
```

Here's how it's working:

- We have an expensiveValue that is calculated using useMemo. This calculation involves looping many times, and can be costly to run on every re-render.
- The expensive operation is only run when the data prop changes, as this is the only dependency.
- The count state will cause the component to re-render, but because the data prop hasn't changed, the expensive function will not be called.

useCallback: Memoizing Functions

The useCallback hook is used to memoize functions. This prevents the function from being re-created on every render, which is especially important when passing down functions as props to child components. This ensures that the child component will not be re-rendered if the function does not change.

Here is the basic syntax:

```
import React, { useCallback } from 'react';

function MyComponent({ onClick }) {
  const memoizedCallback = useCallback(() => {
    // Function logic here
  }, [dependencies]);
  // Use the memoizedCallback
}
```

Here's what's happening:

- useCallback(callback, [dependencies]): Similar to useMemo, useCallback takes two arguments:
    - callback: The function that you want to memoize.
    - [dependencies]: An array of dependencies, which determines when the callback function will be re-created. If any of the dependencies change, then a new function will be created. If no dependencies are provided, then the function will only be created once on mount.

- memoizedCallback: The memoized function that can now be used.

Practical Implementation: Preventing Child Re-Renders

Let's look at an example where we're using useCallback to prevent a child component from re-rendering:

```
import React, { useState, useCallback } from 'react';

function ChildComponent({ onClick }){
    console.log("ChildComponent rendered.")
  return (
    <button onClick={onClick}>Click</button>
  );
}
function ParentComponent(){
    const [count, setCount] = useState(0);
  const handleClick = useCallback(() => {
    setCount(prevCount => prevCount + 1);
  }, []);
  return (
    <div>
        <p>Count: {count}</p>
        <ChildComponent onClick={handleClick} />
    </div>
  );
}
export default ParentComponent;
```

Let's analyze the code:

- The ParentComponent has state that when updated causes it to re-render.
- The handleClick function is wrapped with the useCallback hook, so that the function is not re-created every time the ParentComponent re-renders.
- We pass the handleClick function as the onClick prop to the ChildComponent.
- If we didn't use useCallback, the ChildComponent will re-render every time the ParentComponent re-renders, because the onClick prop would be a new function on each render.
- Now that we're using useCallback, we can see that the child component does not re-render if only the parent component's state is being updated.

Choosing Between useMemo and useCallback

- Use useMemo when you need to prevent expensive calculations from running on every re-render.
- Use useCallback when you need to memoize functions, to prevent components from re-rendering unnecessarily.

Practical Implementation: Combined Use of useMemo and useCallback

Let's create an example where we combine useMemo and useCallback:

```
import React, { useState, useCallback, useMemo } from
'react';

function ChildComponent({ onClick, data }){
   console.log("ChildComponent rendered.")
    return <button onClick={onClick}>Click {data}</button>
}
function ParentComponent(){
    const [count, setCount] = useState(0);
    const expensiveValue = useMemo(() => {
       console.log("expensive calculation");
       let sum = 0;
       for (let i = 0; i < 1000000; i++) {
           sum += count + i;
       }
       return sum;
    }, [count]);
    const handleClick = useCallback(() => {
      setCount(prevCount => prevCount + 1);
    }, []);

    return (
      <div>
        <p>Count: {count}</p>
        <ChildComponent onClick={handleClick} data={expensiveValue}
/>
      </div>
    );
}
export default ParentComponent;
```

Here's the breakdown:

- We have a ParentComponent that has a count state, as well as an expensive computation that is memoized using useMemo.
- We are passing a handleClick function, as well as the result of the expensive calculation (expensiveValue) to the ChildComponent

- The handleClick is memoized using useCallback, so that it is not created on every render.
- If we didn't use useCallback and useMemo, we would see that the ChildComponent re-renders on every re-render.

Personal Insights

I remember when I first started learning React, I didn't understand memoization, and I didn't use these hooks at all. I often found myself trying to optimize my application, but it was difficult to know where the performance bottlenecks were. After learning about memoization, I have found that it's one of the most important techniques that I use to make sure that my applications are performant.

Key Takeaways:

- Memoization is a technique to cache results, and avoid re-rendering unnecessarily.
- useMemo is used to memoize values that result from expensive calculations.
- useCallback is used to memoize functions, to avoid re-creating them on every render.
- Both hooks take in a dependency array, which determines when the function will be re-executed.

By understanding how to use useMemo and useCallback, you'll be able to significantly improve the performance of your React applications, and ensure that they are responsive and fast. These are essential tools in the React developer's toolbox.

8.3 LAZY LOADING AND CODE SPLITTING: LOADING CODE EFFICIENTLY

Lazy loading and code splitting are techniques that allow you to load your application's code only when it is needed, instead of loading everything at once. These techniques help to reduce your application's initial load time, and improve the overall user experience.

Code Splitting: Breaking Down Your Application

Code splitting involves dividing your application into smaller, more manageable chunks that can be loaded on demand. Instead of loading a large monolithic JavaScript file, you're loading multiple smaller ones as they are required.

This helps with:

- **Faster Initial Load Time:** Reduces the amount of code that needs to be downloaded initially, making your application load faster when users visit the website for the first time.
- **Reduced Bandwidth Consumption**: Only the needed code is downloaded.
- **Improved User Experience:** Faster loading translates to a much better user experience.

Lazy Loading: Loading Components on Demand

Lazy loading is a specific implementation of code splitting, where components are loaded only when they are needed, instead of loading them upfront. This is particularly useful for components that are not immediately visible on page load, or that are located on different routes.

Implementing Lazy Loading with React

React provides the lazy function along with the Suspense component to implement lazy loading. The lazy function is used to load a component dynamically, and Suspense is used to display a fallback UI while the component is being loaded.

Here's how you might use lazy loading:

```
import React, { Suspense, lazy } from 'react';

const MyComponent = lazy(() => import('./MyComponent'));

function App(){
    return (
        <Suspense fallback={<p>Loading...</p>}>
            <MyComponent />
        </Suspense>
    );
}
export default App;
```

Here's a breakdown:

1. **lazy() Function**: The lazy function takes a function, that must return a Promise, where the resolved value is the component you want to lazily load.
2. **import() function**: We are using the dynamic import statement, which will load our component from the specified path.
3. **Suspense Component**: The Suspense component is used to wrap the lazy loaded component, and takes in a fallback prop which is used to display a loading message while the component is loading.

This example will load the MyComponent only when it is rendered in the application, instead of loading it initially.

Practical Implementation: Lazy Loading with React Router

Let's see how to use lazy and Suspense in a React Router application, where we are loading a different component depending on the current route.

```jsx
import React, { Suspense, lazy } from 'react';
import { BrowserRouter, Routes, Route, Link } from 'react-router-dom';

const Home = lazy(() => import('./Home'));
const About = lazy(() => import('./About'));
function App(){
    return (
      <BrowserRouter>
        <nav>
          <ul>
            <li><Link to="/">Home</Link></li>
            <li><Link to="/about">About</Link></li>
          </ul>
        </nav>
          <Suspense fallback={<p>Loading...</p>}>
           <Routes>
              <Route path="/" element={<Home />} />
              <Route path="/about" element={<About />} />
           </Routes>
          </Suspense>
      </BrowserRouter>
    );
}
export default App;
```

Here's how we are using lazy loading:

- We are using the lazy function to load the Home, and About components when they are first rendered by React Router. This means that we are only loading the component that the user is currently looking at, rather than loading all of the components upfront.
- We are using the Suspense component, to display a loading message while the component is loading.

With this example, you're now using code splitting and lazy loading to load routes only when they are needed, resulting in a much faster application.

Benefits of Lazy Loading and Code Splitting

- **Faster Initial Load:** Users see content much quicker, as the initial load time is greatly reduced.
- **Improved Performance**: Load times are improved, and the application feels more responsive.
- **Resource Efficiency:** Only the necessary code is downloaded.
- **Better User Experience:** A much better initial user experience with the application feeling more responsive.

Code Splitting with Webpack

Webpack will be used behind the scenes when you are using lazy loading, to split your application's code into different chunks. If you are looking for more control on how your code is split, then you can also use Webpack's code splitting features. This is beyond the scope of this book, but if you are looking for more control, then I would encourage you to look into how to use Webpack's features.

Practical Implementation: Lazy Loading with a Loading Spinner

Let's look at a more practical example of lazy loading, where instead of displaying a paragraph, we're going to display a loading spinner:

```
import React, { Suspense, lazy } from 'react';
import { BrowserRouter, Routes, Route, Link } from 'react-router-dom';
import "./styles.css";
const Home = lazy(() => import('./Home'));
const About = lazy(() => import('./About'));
function LoadingSpinner(){
    return (
        <div className="spinner-container">
            <div className="loading-spinner">
            </div>
```

```jsx
        </div>
    );
}
function App(){
    return (
        <BrowserRouter>
            <nav>
                <ul>
                    <li><Link to="/">Home</Link></li>
                    <li><Link to="/about">About</Link></li>
                </ul>
            </nav>
            <Suspense fallback={<LoadingSpinner />}>
                <Routes>
                    <Route path="/" element={<Home />} />
                    <Route path="/about" element={<About />} />
                </Routes>
            </Suspense>
        </BrowserRouter>
    );
}
export default App;
```

content_copy download
Use code with caution.Jsx
And here are some styles for the loading spinner styles.css:

```css
    .spinner-container {
    display: flex;
    justify-content: center;
    align-items: center;
    height: 100px;
}
.loading-spinner {
    border: 5px solid #f3f3f3; /* Light grey */
    border-top: 5px solid #3498db; /* Blue */
    border-radius: 50%;
    width: 30px;
    height: 30px;
    animation: spin 2s linear infinite;
}

@keyframes spin {
    0% { transform: rotate(0deg); }
    100% { transform: rotate(360deg); }
}
```

In this implementation, we have replaced the fallback paragraph with a loading spinner. This is a much more user-friendly loading indicator.

Personal Insight

When I first started building React applications, I didn't know about code splitting and lazy loading. My applications were always slow to load. Once I implemented lazy loading, I saw a dramatic improvement to the load times of my applications. I highly recommend that you try to use lazy loading in all of your applications.

Key Takeaways:

- Code splitting is where you divide your application into smaller chunks of code, and loading these chunks on demand.
- Lazy loading is when you load components only when they are actually needed. This can be implemented using React's lazy function, combined with Suspense.
- You can use lazy loading with React Router, to load your components only when the user navigates to a specific route.
- Lazy loading improves the performance of your application, by making the initial load time much faster.

By mastering lazy loading and code splitting, you'll be able to build React applications that are not only more performant but also provide a much better experience for your users. These are essential techniques for optimizing web applications.

8.4 SERVER-SIDE RENDERING (SSR) AND STATIC SITE GENERATION (SSG): ENHANCING PERFORMANCE AND SEO

Client-side rendering (CSR) is the default for most React applications, and it is what we have been using throughout this book so far. With client side rendering, the initial HTML that the user receives is empty, and then the javascript will be downloaded and executed, and the components will be rendered on the client side. While CSR is great for many applications, it is not performant for applications that need to load very quickly, or when SEO is an important consideration, because it will take a while before the first paint of your application. This is where Server-Side Rendering (SSR), and Static Site Generation (SSG) come into play. These two techniques move the rendering process from the client's browser to the server, or during the build time.

Server-Side Rendering (SSR): Rendering on the Server

Server-Side Rendering (SSR) is when the application's components are rendered on the server, and then the final HTML is sent to the browser. Instead of the browser having to download all of your javascript and then rendering the application, the user receives HTML and has the ability to see the application almost immediately.

Here are the key benefits of SSR:

- **Faster Initial Load**: With SSR, users see the content almost immediately, because the HTML is already rendered and is sent directly from the server.
- **Better SEO**: Search engines can easily crawl your website because all the content is available in the HTML, as opposed to a client-side rendered application, where the search engine may have to wait for all the javascript to be downloaded and executed.
- **Accessibility**: Improves the experience for users with slow internet connections, or for users that use assistive technology.
- **Dynamic Content:** SSR is great for applications that need to display data that can change very often, and be updated on the server.

Practical Implementation: Setting up SSR with Next.js

While you can implement SSR yourself, it can be very complicated. Frameworks like Next.js can make this process much easier, by providing a lot of features out of the box, as well as an easy way of setting up SSR.

Let's look at a simple example using Next.js.

First, create a new Next.js app:

```
npx create-next-app my-ssr-app
cd my-ssr-app
npm run dev
```

Then navigate to the pages directory, and open up pages/index.js, replace the content with this:

```
import React from 'react';
function Home({ data }) {
    return (
      <div>
        <h1>Welcome to the home page</h1>
          <p>The data is: {data}</p>
```

170

```
      </div>
    )
}
export async function getServerSideProps(){
  const data = "This is data from the server!"
  return {
      props: {
          data
      }
  }
}
export default Home;
```

Here's how it works:

- **getServerSideProps Function**: This special function runs on the server-side, before rendering our component, and can be used to fetch data that will be passed down as props to your component.
- **Fetching Data**: This is where you can make API calls, or fetch data from a database. We are just returning some static data in our example.
- **Returning Props**: The data that you fetch in this function will be passed down as props to your page component.
- **Rendering the Component**: The component will now be rendered on the server side.
- **Start Development Server**: When you run npm run dev, and navigate to your application in your browser, you can see that the content is rendered on the server-side, before sending it to the browser.

Static Site Generation (SSG): Generating HTML at Build Time

With Static Site Generation (SSG), the HTML content is generated at build time, and is then deployed as static HTML files on a server. This is similar to server side rendering, but instead of generating the pages when they are requested, they are generated ahead of time, when you build the application.

Here are some of the benefits of SSG:

- **Extremely Fast Load Times**: HTML files load very quickly, without any overhead.
- **Scalability**: SSG is extremely scalable, because you can host the HTML files on a CDN (Content Delivery Network).
- **Better SEO:** Similar to SSR, search engines can easily crawl SSG sites.

- **Ideal for Static Content**: It is ideal for websites that do not change very often.

Practical Implementation: Implementing SSG with Next.js

Next.js also provides a very simple way of implementing SSG.

Let's modify our previous Next.js code to use SSG:

```
import React from 'react';
function Home({ data }) {
    return (
        <div>
            <h1>Welcome to the home page</h1>
            <p>The data is: {data}</p>
        </div>
    )
}
export async function getStaticProps(){
    const data = "This is data from build time!"
    return {
        props: {
            data
        }
    }
}
export default Home;
```

Here's how it works:

- **getStaticProps Function**: Instead of using the getServerSideProps we are now using getStaticProps. This function is run at the build time.
- **Fetching Data**: We can fetch data here, but in our case we are just returning static data. This data will be used to render our component at build time.
- **Rendering HTML**: When we build our application, using npm run build, the HTML pages will be created from the data returned from the getStaticProps function. This will then be served to the user.

Choosing Between SSR and SSG

- **SSR**: Choose SSR if your application needs to show real time data that is constantly changing.
- **SSG**: Choose SSG if your application is mostly static content, that does not change very often.

Personal Insight

When I first started learning about React, I found it difficult to understand the value of SSR. I thought that client side rendering was good enough. After some time, I realized that SSR and SSG are essential for creating performant websites. Now, I always try to use a framework that enables SSR/SSG for all of my public facing web applications.

Key Takeaways:

- Server-Side Rendering (SSR) renders the HTML on the server and sends the HTML to the browser, resulting in a faster load time.
- Static Site Generation (SSG) generates the HTML at build time, and allows you to serve static HTML files.
- Both SSR and SSG can be used to drastically improve the performance, SEO, and accessibility of your website.
- SSR is used for sites that display data that changes often, while SSG is used for websites that mostly display static content.

By understanding SSR and SSG, you'll be able to build much more performant and scalable React applications. These skills are essential for any developer, especially when building large scale applications.

CHAPTER 9: TESTING REACT APPLICATIONS

Testing is a fundamental part of software development, and React applications are no exception. Writing tests will help you find bugs, and make sure that your code is doing what it is supposed to do. In this chapter, we'll explore different types of testing that you can implement, from unit tests to end-to-end testing.

9.1 UNIT TESTING WITH JEST AND REACT TESTING LIBRARY: TESTING IN ISOLATION

Unit testing involves testing individual units of code in isolation. In React, this typically means testing individual components, functions, or hooks in a way that does not rely on other components or parts of your application. This approach will help you identify bugs early on, and also will help to create more maintainable and modular applications. Jest is a popular testing framework, and React Testing Library is a library that encourages you to test components in a user-centric way, by testing what the user sees instead of the internal state of your components.

Setting up Jest and React Testing Library

Before we begin, we need to install Jest and React Testing Library using npm:

```
npm install --save-dev jest @testing-library/react @testing-library/jest-dom
```

Here's what the packages do:

- jest: A testing framework with a rich API, and also comes with a built in test runner.
- @testing-library/react: A library for rendering and interacting with React components in your test.
- @testing-library/jest-dom: Provides custom Jest matchers for making assertions on the state of the DOM.

Next, configure Jest in your package.json by adding a test script:

```
"scripts": {
```

```
    "test": "jest"
  }
```

Create a jest.config.js file in your project root directory:

```
    module.exports = {
    testEnvironment: "jsdom",
    setupFilesAfterEnv: ["<rootDir>/jest.setup.js"]
};
```

And lastly, create jest.setup.js file in your project root directory:

```
    import '@testing-library/jest-dom';
```

This setupFilesAfterEnv file is used to import @testing-library/jest-dom, and add all its custom matchers to your Jest environment.

Writing Your First Unit Test

Let's start with a very basic example. We'll create a component that renders a message, and then test that component to make sure it renders the correct text.

MyComponent.jsx:

```
    import React from 'react';
function MyComponent({ message }){
  return <p>{message}</p>;
}
export default MyComponent;
```

Here's the corresponding test, MyComponent.test.jsx:

```
    import React from 'react';
import { render, screen } from '@testing-library/react';
import MyComponent from './MyComponent';

test('renders the component with correct message', () => {
    render(<MyComponent message="Hello World!" />);
    const messageElement = screen.getByText('Hello World!');
    expect(messageElement).toBeInTheDocument();
});
```

Let's walk through the code step by step:

1. **Importing modules**: We are importing render, and screen from @testing-library/react, as well as our component MyComponent from the corresponding component file.
2. **Test Definition**: We use the test function to start a new test. The test function takes in a string that will be used as the name of the test, and also a callback function that will contain our test code.
3. **Rendering the Component**: We are using the render function from React Testing Library, to render our component into a virtual DOM environment. We also pass a message prop to our component.
4. **Querying Elements:** We use the screen object, to get a reference to our element that has the text Hello World!.
5. **Assertion:** Lastly we are using the Jest's expect function, as well as the toBeInTheDocument method from @testing-library/jest-dom, to assert that the message element is present in the virtual DOM.

To run this test, run the command npm run test. If your test passes, then you will see that your test has been successful.

Testing User Interactions

Let's take this a step further and test components that interact with the user. We will now test a component that has a button, and updates the text on the screen when the button is clicked.

ButtonComponent.jsx:

```
import React, { useState } from 'react';
function ButtonComponent() {
  const [message, setMessage] = useState("Hello");
    function handleClick(){
       setMessage("Button Clicked!")
    }
  return (
    <div>
     <p>{message}</p>
     <button onClick={handleClick}>Click Me</button>
    </div>
  );
}
export default ButtonComponent;
```

And here's the corresponding test: ButtonComponent.test.jsx

```jsx
import React from 'react';
import { render, screen, fireEvent } from '@testing-library/react';
import ButtonComponent from './ButtonComponent';
test('updates message when button is clicked', () => {
    render(<ButtonComponent />);
    const buttonElement = screen.getByRole('button', { name: 'Click
Me' });
    const messageElement = screen.getByText('Hello');
    fireEvent.click(buttonElement);
    expect(messageElement).toHaveTextContent('Button Clicked!');
});
```

Let's walk through the code:

1. **Importing Modules:** We are importing render, screen, and fireEvent from @testing-library/react.
2. **Rendering the Component:** We are rendering the component using render, to display the component in the virtual DOM.
3. **Getting Elements:** We are using getByRole to get the button by its role, and we are using getByText, to get the message element, and then store them in variables.
4. **Simulating User Action:** We are simulating the user clicking the button using fireEvent.click.
5. **Assertion:** Finally we are asserting that the message element now has the text "Button Clicked!", which confirms that our component has behaved correctly.

Testing Component Logic

Let's look at another example, where we're testing a simple counter:

Counter.jsx:

```jsx
import React, { useState } from 'react';
function Counter() {
    const [count, setCount] = useState(0);
    function increment(){
        setCount(prevCount => prevCount + 1);
    }
    return (
        <div>
            <p>Count: {count}</p>
            <button onClick={increment}>Increment</button>
```

```
        </div>
    );
}
export default Counter;
```

Here's the corresponding test file Counter.test.jsx:

```
        import React from 'react';
import { render, screen, fireEvent } from '@testing-library/react';
import Counter from './Counter';
test('increments the counter when button is clicked', () => {
    render(<Counter />);
    const buttonElement = screen.getByRole('button', { name:
'Increment' });
    const countElement = screen.getByText(/Count: 0/i);
    fireEvent.click(buttonElement);
    expect(countElement).toHaveTextContent('Count: 1');
});
```

Here's the breakdown:

- **Getting Elements**: We are getting the button element using getByRole, and the initial value of the counter using getByText. We are using a regular expression to get the text, so that it is more robust to changes, if we were to change the text from Count: 0 to Count: 0 items.
- **Simulating Click:** We are using fireEvent to simulate a click.
- **Assertion:** Finally we are asserting that the counter element now has the correct value.

Practical Implementation: Testing a Component with Multiple Elements

Let's create a component that displays a list of items, and test that it displays all of the items that we expect.

ListComponent.jsx:

```
        import React from 'react';
function ListComponent({ items }){
    return (
        <ul>
            {items.map(item => (
            <li key={item}>{item}</li>
            ))}
        </ul>
```

```
      );
}
export default ListComponent;
```

And its corresponding test: ListComponent.test.jsx:

```
    import React from 'react';
import { render, screen } from '@testing-library/react';
import ListComponent from './ListComponent';
test('renders a list of items', () => {
    const items = ['item 1', 'item 2', 'item 3'];
    render(<ListComponent items={items} />);
    const listItems = screen.getAllByRole('listitem');
  expect(listItems).toHaveLength(items.length);
  items.forEach(item => {
        expect(screen.getByText(item)).toBeInTheDocument();
  });
});
```

Here's what's happening:

- We are using render to render our component into a virtual DOM.
- We are also passing in the props that we expect the component to receive.
- We use the getAllByRole function to get all elements with the role listitem, which will correspond to our <li> elements.
- We are asserting that the length of the list items is the same as the length of our items prop.
- Then we are using forEach, to ensure that the text inside each li matches what we expect.

Personal Insights

When I first started learning about testing in React, it felt like a huge burden, and I didn't really see the value of writing tests. Now after several years of building React applications, I can see how valuable testing is to ensure that your application is robust, and has a very minimal number of bugs. I have found React Testing Library to be extremely valuable, because it allows you to write tests from the perspective of a user, rather than testing implementation details.

Key Takeaways:

- Unit tests verify individual components or functions in isolation, to ensure that they work correctly.

- Jest is the most popular testing framework for Javascript, and is used for running your tests.
- React Testing Library encourages you to test components from the perspective of the user, by focusing on how the component interacts with the DOM.
- You can use render, screen, and fireEvent from React Testing Library to render your components, get elements from the DOM, and simulate user events.
- Writing unit tests is the foundation for ensuring that your application is working as expected.

By understanding how to write unit tests with Jest and React Testing Library, you'll be well-equipped to start writing robust and maintainable React applications. Testing should be the cornerstone of your development process.

9.2 TESTING HOOKS AND ASYNCHRONOUS LOGIC: ENSURING FUNCTIONALITY

Testing Hooks and asynchronous logic can be a little more involved than testing regular components. Hooks have no UI, and they do not directly render any jsx. Asynchronous code, by nature, is not synchronous, which means you cannot always guarantee the order that your tests will run in. Therefore, it requires specific techniques to ensure that your tests are reliable and cover all the edge cases. Let's explore how we can use Jest and React Testing Library to solve these problems.

Testing Hooks with React Testing Library

It's important to know that React Testing Library is not designed to test hooks directly, as it is a library that encourages testing from the perspective of the user, and testing components through their DOM elements. Hooks do not render any DOM elements, so we will need to test them by creating a component that uses the hook.

Let's create a custom hook called useCounter that we want to test:

useCounter.js:

```
import { useState } from 'react';
function useCounter(initialValue = 0) {
    const [count, setCount] = useState(initialValue);
    function increment() {
```

```
        setCount(prevCount => prevCount + 1);
    }
  function decrement() {
        setCount(prevCount => prevCount - 1);
    }
    return {
        count,
        increment,
        decrement
    };
}
export default useCounter;
```

Here's a simple component that uses this hook CounterComponent.jsx:

```
        import React from 'react';
import useCounter from "./useCounter";
function CounterComponent(){
  const { count, increment, decrement } = useCounter();
    return (
        <div>
            <p>Count: {count}</p>
              <button onClick={increment}>Increment</button>
              <button onClick={decrement}>Decrement</button>
        </div>
    );
}
export default CounterComponent;
```

And the corresponding test CounterComponent.test.jsx:

```
        import React from 'react';
import { render, screen, fireEvent } from '@testing-library/react';
import CounterComponent from './CounterComponent';

test('increments and decrements the counter', () => {
    render(<CounterComponent />);
    const incrementButton = screen.getByRole('button', { name:
'Increment' });
    const decrementButton = screen.getByRole('button', { name:
'Decrement' });
    const countElement = screen.getByText(/Count: 0/i);

    fireEvent.click(incrementButton);
    expect(countElement).toHaveTextContent('Count: 1');

    fireEvent.click(decrementButton);
    expect(countElement).toHaveTextContent('Count: 0');
```

```
});
```

Here's what we're doing:

- We create a simple component that uses the custom hook.
- We are rendering the component using the render function, and then grabbing elements from the component using getByRole and getByText.
- We are simulating user interactions, using fireEvent, to click the buttons, and then asserting that the counter changes correctly.

Testing Asynchronous Logic with Jest

Testing asynchronous logic can be tricky, but with Jest, it is possible to write reliable tests that cover all the different use cases. When testing asynchronous logic, you will need to mock any external dependencies, such as the fetch API, or an API call.

Let's take a look at an example of how we can test an asynchronous operation, where we will test a function that makes a request to an API using the fetch API.

Here is our function fetchData.js:

```
const fetchData = async () => {
  const response = await
fetch('https://jsonplaceholder.typicode.com/todos/1');
  if (!response.ok) {
    throw new Error("Failed to fetch data")
  }
  return await response.json();
}
export default fetchData;
```

And the corresponding test fetchData.test.js:

```
import fetchData from "./fetchData";
test('fetches data successfully', async () => {
    global.fetch = jest.fn(() =>
        Promise.resolve({
            ok: true,
            json: () => Promise.resolve({ title: 'Test Todo' }),
        })
    );
    const data = await fetchData();
```

```
    expect(data.title).toEqual('Test Todo');
});

test('fails to fetch data', async () => {
  global.fetch = jest.fn(() =>
      Promise.resolve({
          ok: false,
      })
  );
    await expect(fetchData()).rejects.toThrow('Failed to fetch
data');
});
```

Let's break down our testing code:

1. **Mocking fetch:** Before making our API call, we are mocking the fetch API.
   o   jest.fn will create a mock function that can be used instead of our real fetch function.
   o   We are also setting it up, to return a resolved promise that contains the data that we expect our json() function to return.
2. **async/await:** We use async to make sure the test function is asynchronous, and then use await to wait for the result of our asynchronous function.
3. **Success Assertion:** After the fetchData function returns its result, we can now make assertions based on that data, by making sure the title property matches what we expected.
4. **Error Assertion:** For our second test, we are creating another mock function, but this time, it returns a rejected promise, which will allow us to test the error state. We are expecting that the function will throw the correct error message using expect(...).rejects.toThrow().

With this technique, we can effectively test all our asynchronous operations, as well as handle edge cases for errors.

Practical Implementation: Testing a Component with Asynchronous Logic

Let's look at an example of a component that fetches data using the fetch API, and use all of our new techniques to ensure that this component is working correctly.

DataComponent.jsx:

```
    import React, { useState, useEffect } from 'react';
const DataComponent = ({ url }) => {
  const [data, setData] = useState(null);
  const [loading, setLoading] = useState(true);
```

```jsx
  const [error, setError] = useState(null);
  useEffect(() => {
    async function fetchData(){
        try {
           const response = await fetch(url);
           if (!response.ok) {
              throw new Error("Failed to fetch data");
           }
           const result = await response.json();
           setData(result);
        } catch (err) {
          setError(err.message);
        } finally {
          setLoading(false);
        }
    }
     fetchData();
  }, [url])
  if (loading) return <p>Loading...</p>;
  if (error) return <p>Error: {error}</p>;
   if(!data) return <p>No Data!</p>;
    return (
      <p>Title: {data.title}</p>
    );
};
export default DataComponent;
```

And the corresponding test DataComponent.test.jsx:

```jsx
      import React from 'react';
import { render, screen, waitFor } from '@testing-library/react';
import DataComponent from "./DataComponent";
test('fetches data successfully and displays the title', async ()
=> {
    global.fetch = jest.fn(() =>
        Promise.resolve({
           ok: true,
            json: () => Promise.resolve({ title: 'Test Todo' }),
        })
    );
    render(<DataComponent url="test-url" />);
    const titleElement = await waitFor(() =>
screen.getByText('Title: Test Todo'));
  expect(titleElement).toBeInTheDocument();
});
test('fails to fetch data and displays the error message', async ()
=> {
    global.fetch = jest.fn(() =>
        Promise.resolve({
```

```
        ok: false,
      })
    );
    render(<DataComponent url="test-url" />);
    const errorElement = await waitFor(() =>
screen.getByText('Error: Failed to fetch data'));
    expect(errorElement).toBeInTheDocument();
});
test('displays loading message while fetching data', () => {
  global.fetch = jest.fn(() => new Promise(() => {}));
    render(<DataComponent url="test-url" />);
  const loadingElement = screen.getByText('Loading...');
  expect(loadingElement).toBeInTheDocument();
});
```

Let's walk through our code:

- We are mocking our fetch requests using jest.fn, and returning our promise to mimic a successful, and also a failed API response.
- We are using the render method to render our component.
- We are using the waitFor function from React Testing Library to await for a specific element to appear, indicating that our asynchronous action has completed.
- We then assert that the correct message is rendered in our tests.
- Lastly we are checking our loading message, to make sure that we display a loading indicator.

Personal Insight

When I first started testing my React components, I had no idea how to test hooks and asynchronous logic, and it was extremely challenging to test these. Now, I find it much easier to test these parts of the application by using the techniques that we have covered here. I think that using React Testing Library to test components based on the user interaction, rather than focusing on implementation details makes testing much simpler and more effective.

Key Takeaways:

- React Testing Library is designed to test components by interacting with the DOM, rather than testing implementation details. Therefore it is best to test hooks using a component.
- You can use Jest's mock functions to mock out any external dependencies, such as API calls, and mock the results.

- Use async/await to manage asynchronous operations in your tests.
- waitFor from React Testing Library can be used to wait for components to be updated after an asynchronous action has completed.

By understanding how to test hooks and asynchronous logic, you can create much more robust and maintainable React applications. These are essential skills to learn when building any modern React application.

9.3 COMPONENT AND INTEGRATION TESTING: ENSURING INTEROPERABILITY

While unit tests are a fundamental part of testing, they only test single units of code in isolation. To ensure that your application is working properly, you need to also test multiple parts of your code working together, which is the goal of component and integration tests. Component tests are more concerned with testing multiple components working together, while integration tests often involve testing data flow between different parts of your application. These tests are important for catching bugs that may occur when your different components or modules are working together.

Component Testing with React Testing Library

Component tests focus on testing multiple components working together, typically within a single component tree. This verifies that your component is working correctly with its child components.

Let's take a look at an example of a ParentComponent and its child component ChildComponent.

ChildComponent.jsx:

```
import React from 'react';
function ChildComponent({ message }) {
    return (
        <p>{message}</p>
    );
}
export default ChildComponent;
```

ParentComponent.jsx:

186

```
    import React from 'react';
import ChildComponent from "./ChildComponent";

function ParentComponent(){
   return (
       <div>
           <h1>Parent Component</h1>
           <ChildComponent message="Hello from parent!" />
       </div>
   );
}
export default ParentComponent;
```

And here is its corresponding test, ParentComponent.test.jsx:

```
    import React from 'react';
import { render, screen } from '@testing-library/react';
import ParentComponent from './ParentComponent';

test('renders parent and child components', () => {
    render(<ParentComponent />);
    const parentText = screen.getByText('Parent Component');
  const childText = screen.getByText('Hello from parent!');
   expect(parentText).toBeInTheDocument();
    expect(childText).toBeInTheDocument();
});
```

Here's how we are testing it:

- We are using render, to render the ParentComponent, which also renders its child components.
- We are then using getByText, to check that the parent and child components are rendered correctly, based on text that is displayed by the component.

With this test, we are testing that the ParentComponent is rendered correctly, as well as that it is also rendering its child component correctly.

Practical Implementation: Testing Component Interactions

Let's expand on our previous example and test how components interact with each other, using event listeners.

ChildComponent.jsx:

```jsx
import React from 'react';
function ChildComponent({ onClick, message }) {
  return (
    <button onClick={onClick}>{message}</button>
  );
}
export default ChildComponent;
```

ParentComponent.jsx:

```jsx
import React, { useState } from 'react';
import ChildComponent from "./ChildComponent";

function ParentComponent(){
    const [count, setCount] = useState(0);
    function handleClick(){
        setCount(prevCount => prevCount + 1);
    }
  return (
    <div>
        <h1>Parent Component</h1>
        <p>Count: {count}</p>
        <ChildComponent onClick={handleClick} message="Click me!" />
    </div>
  );
}
export default ParentComponent;
```

And here's our test ParentComponent.test.jsx:

```jsx
import React from 'react';
import { render, screen, fireEvent } from '@testing-library/react';
import ParentComponent from './ParentComponent';

test('updates the parent state when the child button is clicked',
() => {
    render(<ParentComponent />);
    const buttonElement = screen.getByRole('button', { name: "Click
me!" });
    const countElement = screen.getByText(/Count: 0/i);
    fireEvent.click(buttonElement);
    expect(countElement).toHaveTextContent("Count: 1");
});
```

Here's what we're doing:

- We are rendering the ParentComponent, which also renders the ChildComponent.
- We are using getByRole to get the button in the child component, and getByText to get the count in the parent component.
- We are then using fireEvent to simulate a click on the button.
- Lastly, we are asserting that the count in the parent component now has the text "Count: 1", showing that the parent and child component is communicating correctly.

Integration Testing: Testing Data Flow

Integration testing is focused on testing the data flow between different components. These tests will often involve multiple components, as well as mocking external dependencies.

Let's create an example where we have a ParentComponent that has an input field, and a ChildComponent, that displays the current value of the input.

ChildComponent.jsx:

```
import React from 'react';
function ChildComponent({ message }){
    return (
        <p>{message}</p>
    );
}
export default ChildComponent;
```

ParentComponent.jsx:

```
import React, { useState } from 'react';
import ChildComponent from "./ChildComponent";

function ParentComponent(){
    const [text, setText] = useState('');
    function handleInputChange(e){
        setText(e.target.value)
    }
    return (
        <div>
            <h1>Parent Component</h1>
            <input type="text" value={text}
onChange={handleInputChange} />
```

```
        <ChildComponent message={text} />
      </div>
  );
}
export default ParentComponent;
```

And the corresponding test ParentComponent.test.jsx:

```
    import React from 'react';
import { render, screen, fireEvent } from '@testing-library/react';
import ParentComponent from "./ParentComponent";
test('updates child component when input is changed', () => {
    render(<ParentComponent />);
    const inputElement = screen.getByRole('textbox');
    const childElement = screen.getByText('');

    fireEvent.change(inputElement, { target: { value: 'Hello!' }
});
  expect(childElement).toHaveTextContent('Hello!');
});
```

Here's what's happening:

- We're rendering the ParentComponent, which also renders the ChildComponent.
- We are then getting the input element from the parent component, and also the p element from the ChildComponent.
- We are then using fireEvent to simulate a change event in the input field.
- And then we assert that the child component now has the text "Hello!".

With this test, we are ensuring that the parent component is correctly passing data to the child component.

Practical Implementation: Testing API Calls

Let's take the previous example a step further, and introduce an API call to test how all of the components interact with asynchronous data.

ChildComponent.jsx:

```
    import React, { useState, useEffect } from 'react';
import axios from 'axios';
function ChildComponent({ userId }) {
```

```jsx
    const [user, setUser] = useState(null);
    useEffect(() => {
      async function getUser() {
          const result = await
axios.get(`https://jsonplaceholder.typicode.com/users/${userId}`);
          setUser(result.data);
      }
      getUser();
    }, [userId])
    if (!user) return <p>Loading User...</p>
    return (
    <p>User: {user.name}</p>
    );
}
export default ChildComponent;
```

ParentComponent.jsx:

```jsx
    import React from 'react';
import ChildComponent from "./ChildComponent";
function ParentComponent(){
    return (
      <div>
        <h1>Parent Component</h1>
          <ChildComponent userId={1} />
      </div>
    )
}
export default ParentComponent;
```

And the corresponding test ParentComponent.test.jsx:

```jsx
    import React from 'react';
import { render, screen, waitFor } from '@testing-library/react';
import ParentComponent from "./ParentComponent";
import axios from 'axios';

jest.mock('axios');
test('fetches user data and renders it in the child component',
async () => {
  axios.get.mockResolvedValue({ data: { name: 'John Doe' } });
  render(<ParentComponent />);
    const userElement = await waitFor(() => screen.getByText('User:
John Doe'));
    expect(userElement).toBeInTheDocument();
});
```

Here's the breakdown:

- We are mocking the axios library using jest.mock('axios'), to prevent making API calls when running tests.
- We are also mocking the return value of the axios get method, so that we control the data that is returned by the function.
- Lastly we are using waitFor to wait for the asynchronous action to complete, and then assert that the correct data is rendered on the screen.

Key Differences Between Component and Integration Tests

- **Component Tests:** Tests multiple components working together, often testing one single feature of your application.
- **Integration Tests:** Tests multiple components as well as external dependencies, and often tests the entire system, and how data flows between different parts of your application.

Personal Insight

When I first started testing React applications, I had a hard time understanding the difference between component and integration tests, and often wrote tests that were trying to do too much, which made my tests more difficult to maintain. I have since then come to realize that unit tests are for testing small units of logic, components tests are used to test multiple components working together, and that integration tests are for testing multiple parts of an application working together, including external dependencies. This approach to testing is what I often use today, and it is what I recommend you use as well.

Key Takeaways:

- Component tests focus on testing multiple components working together, usually in the context of a single component tree.
- Integration tests are used to test the data flow between multiple components, as well as how components interact with external dependencies.
- Using both component and integration tests will ensure that your application is working correctly when all of the parts are put together.

By understanding how to write both component and integration tests, you will be able to ensure that your application is not only working at a granular level, but that it also works when all the pieces are put together. This is crucial for creating robust applications.

9.4 END-TO-END TESTING WITH CYPRESS: SIMULATING USER INTERACTIONS

End-to-end testing (E2E) is a type of testing that focuses on testing your application from the perspective of the end user. This type of test often involves testing multiple parts of your application together, including the UI, and even server side data. E2E tests will often simulate user interactions using an actual browser, providing a robust way to test your application. Cypress is one of the most popular frameworks for writing E2E tests, and it is very popular in the React community.

Setting Up Cypress

To get started with Cypress, you will need to first install it:

```
npm install cypress --save-dev
```

Next, add a script to your package.json to run Cypress:

```
"scripts": {
  "cypress": "cypress open"
}
```

Now you can open the Cypress test runner with the command:

```
npm run cypress
```

Cypress will then open the test runner in the browser.

Writing Your First Cypress Test

Let's start by creating a simple test to make sure that you have setup Cypress correctly.

Navigate to your cypress directory and create a new directory e2e. Inside of e2e create a new file my-test.cy.js.

```
describe('My First Test', () => {
  it('Visits the Kitchen Sink', () => {
```

193

```
      cy.visit('https://example.cypress.io');
      cy.contains('type').click();
      cy.url().should('include', '/commands/actions')
   })
})
```

Let's go through the code step by step:

1. **describe Block**: The describe function is used to create a test suite. The string "My First Test" will be displayed as the name of our test suite.
2. **it Block**: The it function is used to create a single test, and it also accepts a string which will be used as the name of that test.
3. **cy.visit():** The cy.visit() function navigates the browser to the specified URL.
4. **cy.contains() and .click():** The cy.contains function is used to get an element that contains the given text and then the .click() is used to click that element.
5. **cy.url() and .should():** The cy.url() function gets the current URL, and we are using the .should() method to assert that the URL includes /commands/actions.

If you run the tests, you should see that our test has successfully passed.

Testing User Flows

Let's create a more realistic example that tests the user flows of our application. We will create a simple login form and test the behavior of the login and logout button, and that we navigate to the correct pages.

First, let's set up a simple login and dashboard page, using React Router:

App.jsx:

```
    import React, { useState, createContext, useContext } from
'react';
import { BrowserRouter, Routes, Route, Link, useNavigate, Navigate
} from 'react-router-dom';

const AuthContext = createContext(null);

function AuthProvider({ children }) {
    const [isLoggedIn, setIsLoggedIn] = useState(false);
    const login = () => setIsLoggedIn(true);
    const logout = () => setIsLoggedIn(false);
```

```jsx
    return (
        <AuthContext.Provider value={{ isLoggedIn, login, logout
}}>
            {children}
        </AuthContext.Provider>
    );
}
function useAuth() {
    return useContext(AuthContext);
}
function ProtectedRoute({ children }) {
    const { isLoggedIn } = useAuth();
    if (!isLoggedIn) {
        return <Navigate to="/login" />;
    }
    return children;
}
function Dashboard() {
    const { logout } = useAuth();
    return (
        <div>
          <h1>Dashboard</h1>
            <button onClick={logout}>Logout</button>
        </div>
    );
}
function Login() {
  const { login } = useAuth();
  const navigate = useNavigate();
 function handleLogin() {
      login();
       navigate("/dashboard");
    }
   return (
     <div>
      <h1>Login Page</h1>
       <button onClick={handleLogin}>Login</button>
      </div>
   );
}
function App() {
  return (
    <BrowserRouter>
      <AuthProvider>
            <nav>
                <ul>
                  <li><Link to="/">Home</Link></li>
                    <li><Link to="/dashboard">Dashboard</Link></li>
                </ul>
              </nav>
              <Routes>
```

```
            <Route path="/" element={<h1>Home Page</h1>} />
            <Route path="/login" element={<Login />} />
            <Route path="/dashboard" element={
              <ProtectedRoute>
                  <Dashboard />
              </ProtectedRoute>
            }
          />
        </Routes>
      </AuthProvider>
    </BrowserRouter>
  );
}
export default App;
```

And here's the corresponding Cypress test: login-test.cy.js:

```
describe('Login Flow', () => {
  it('allows a user to log in and out', () => {
      cy.visit('http://localhost:5173/login');
      cy.contains('Login').click();
      cy.url().should('include', '/dashboard');
      cy.contains('Logout').click();
      cy.url().should('include', '/login');
  });
  it('redirects to login if user is not authenticated', () => {
    cy.visit('http://localhost:5173/dashboard');
    cy.url().should('include', '/login');
  });
});
```

Here's what we're doing:

- We are using the cy.visit function to navigate to different URLs.
- We are using the cy.contains to find elements on the screen.
- We are using .click to click an element on the screen.
- And finally, we use cy.url to assert that the URL matches the state that we expect.

Practical Implementation: Testing Complex Data Flows

Let's expand on the previous example, where we are going to make an API call to get a list of users, and then also test the data flow of our application.

Dashboard.jsx:

```
    import React, { useState, useEffect } from 'react';
import { useAuth } from "./App";
import axios from "axios";

function Dashboard(){
  const { logout } = useAuth();
    const [users, setUsers] = useState(null);
  useEffect(() => {
    async function fetchUsers(){
        const result = await
axios.get("https://jsonplaceholder.typicode.com/users");
        setUsers(result.data);
    }
    fetchUsers();
    }, [])
  if(!users) return <p>Loading Users...</p>
  return (
        <div>
          <h1>Dashboard</h1>
           <ul>
             {users.map(user => (
                 <li key={user.id}>{user.name}</li>
             ))}
           </ul>
             <button onClick={logout}>Logout</button>
        </div>
    );
}
export default Dashboard;
```

And here's the corresponding test dashboard-test.cy.js:

```
    describe('Dashboard Flow', () => {
    it('allows a user to log in, fetch the user data, and log out',
() => {
        cy.visit('http://localhost:5173/login');
      cy.intercept('GET',
'https://jsonplaceholder.typicode.com/users', {
          body: [
              {id: 1, name: 'John Doe'},
              {id: 2, name: 'Jane Smith'},
          ],
          statusCode: 200
      }).as('getUsers');

      cy.contains('Login').click();
      cy.wait('@getUsers');
    cy.url().should('include', '/dashboard');
      cy.contains('John Doe').should('be.visible');
```

```
        cy.contains('Jane Smith').should('be.visible');
        cy.contains('Logout').click();
        cy.url().should('include', '/login');
    });
});
```

Here's how we're testing this:

- **Mocking API Calls:** We use the cy.intercept command to intercept the API call and mock the response by returning a list of users.
- **Waiting for API Call:** We use cy.wait('@getUsers') to wait until the mocked API call returns. This will ensure that our test waits for the API call to complete, before making any assertions on the data.
- **Assertions**: Then we use Cypress commands, such as cy.contains and .should('be.visible'), to assert that the data that was returned by the API, is being rendered on the page.
- We then simulate a user logging out, and then assert that we are on the login page.

Personal Insight

I remember when I first started using Cypress, I had a hard time understanding how powerful it was. I was also used to testing small parts of my application at a time, and didn't realize how important it was to test the end-to-end user flows. Once I started implementing E2E tests, I realized how many bugs I was missing. Now I always try to write E2E tests for my applications to catch bugs before my users do.

Key Takeaways:

- End-to-end (E2E) testing tests your application from the perspective of the user in a browser.
- Cypress is a popular framework for implementing E2E tests in React applications.
- You can use cy.visit, cy.contains, and cy.click to interact with elements in the browser.
- You can use cy.intercept to mock API calls and control the data that is returned.
- E2E testing will help you create a robust application that works as expected from the user's perspective.

By mastering E2E testing with Cypress, you'll be able to create much more robust and user-friendly applications, by ensuring that the entire system works as expected. This is essential for any application that is being used by a large number of users.

CHAPTER 10: DEPLOYING AND SCALING REACT APPLICATIONS

Deploying and scaling React applications is a critical part of the development process. In this chapter, we will explore the different options that you can use for hosting your application, as well as how to setup CI/CD pipelines, and also how to make sure your application performs well in production. This chapter will give you the tools you need to create robust, scalable, and reliable applications.

10.1 HOSTING REACT APPS ON VERCEL, NETLIFY, AND AWS: A PRACTICAL GUIDE

When it comes to deploying your React applications, you have a number of great hosting options available to you. Each platform offers unique features and benefits, and knowing which one to choose depends on your specific needs. We'll focus on Vercel, Netlify, and AWS, which are three of the most popular and reliable options for hosting React applications.

Vercel: The Developer-Friendly Choice

Vercel is a platform that's purpose-built for frontend deployments, and it is often the go-to platform for hosting React applications. It prides itself on its simplicity, performance, and developer experience. If you want to deploy your React application without worrying about the intricacies of server configurations, then Vercel is a great option.

Key features of Vercel:

- **Zero-Configuration Deployments:** Vercel often auto-detects your project's settings, minimizing the setup required, which greatly reduces the learning curve.
- **Global CDN:** It comes with a built in global CDN, which reduces latency for users that are far away from the origin server.
- **Serverless Functions:** You can also implement serverless functions to create your backend APIs.
- **Automatic Updates**: Whenever you push code to your repository, it automatically deploys the application.

- **Preview Deployments:** It also allows you to create preview deployments, which are versions of your website, that are only accessible by people that have the url. This is very useful when you are collaborating with a team, as you can easily share changes.

Deploying to Vercel: A Step-by-Step Guide

Let's go through the practical steps required to deploy a React application to Vercel:

1. **Create a Vercel Account**: Head over to the Vercel website and create an account using your email or your social logins.
2. **Import Your Git Repository:** After creating an account, you will be prompted to create a new project. Here you'll need to connect your Git repository from GitHub, GitLab, or Bitbucket.
3. **Configure Your Project:** Vercel is very good at detecting that you are using a React application, and it will automatically configure the build settings for you.
   - Usually the build command is npm run build or yarn build.
   - Usually the output directory is build or dist.
   - However you are also able to configure these manually, if you need to use a different configuration.
4. **Deploy Your Application:** Click the deploy button, and Vercel will automatically build and deploy your application.

With that, your React application is now live, and you can access it through the URL provided by Vercel. Whenever you push changes to the main branch of your repository, it will also automatically re-deploy your application. Vercel has drastically improved the way that we deploy frontend applications, and is an excellent option for any React developer.

Netlify: Flexibility and Integrations

Netlify is another very popular platform that offers many of the same features as Vercel, but it is often seen as more versatile with various integrations. It is a great platform for deploying a large range of websites and applications.

Key features of Netlify:

- **Git Integration:** Provides a very smooth integration with Git repositories such as GitHub, GitLab, and Bitbucket.

- **Continuous Deployment:** When you connect a Git repository to your application, Netlify will automatically rebuild and redeploy your website on each push.
- **Serverless Functions:** Netlify supports serverless functions, where you can write your backend code.
- **Form Handling:** Provides form handling tools, which are very useful for building contact forms, or any form that needs to submit data.
- **Split Testing:** It also offers split testing, which you can use to test different versions of your application.

Deploying to Netlify: A Step-by-Step Guide

Here's how you would deploy your React application to Netlify:

1. **Create a Netlify Account:** Navigate to the Netlify website and create an account using your email or social login.
2. **Import your Git Repository:** Netlify will prompt you to create a new project, and connect your Git repository from GitHub, GitLab, or Bitbucket.
3. **Configure Your Project**: Netlify will often detect that it is a React application, but sometimes you will have to configure the build settings yourself.
   - The build command is usually npm run build or yarn build.
   - The publish directory is usually build or dist.
4. **Deploy:** Netlify will build and deploy your application based on your configurations.

Once the deployment process completes, your React application will be live and accessible via a Netlify-provided URL. Similar to Vercel, this process is fully automated and Netlify will automatically redeploy your application whenever you push to your git repository. Netlify is also an excellent alternative to Vercel, and you can pick this as an option if you find that you need more configurability.

AWS: Flexibility and Scalability

AWS (Amazon Web Services) is a comprehensive cloud platform that offers a huge amount of different services. You can use it for hosting frontend applications, server side applications, databases, and much more. AWS provides a much more flexible way of deploying your application, and allows you to have much more control over your infrastructure.

Key Features of AWS:

- **Scalability:** Provides unmatched scalability, and allows you to scale your application based on user traffic.
- **Flexibility:** Provides a lot of flexibility, as you can fully configure your infrastructure based on your unique requirements.
- **Comprehensive Services:** You have access to a wide variety of different services for any use case.
- **Granular Control:** You have a much more granular control over the entire deployment process, with many different configurable options.
- **Complexity**: Setting up and configuring AWS is often much more complex than using platforms like Vercel or Netlify, and requires more experience to setup and manage.

Deploying to AWS: A Step-by-Step Guide

Let's explore one of the most common methods of deploying a React application using S3 and CloudFront:

1. **Create an AWS Account**: Go to the AWS website and create an account, using your email, or a social login.
2. **Create an S3 Bucket**: Search for S3 in the AWS console, and create a new S3 bucket. Make sure the bucket name is the same as your domain name, if you have one.
3. **Configure S3 Bucket**: Configure the S3 bucket to allow public access, and set the Index Document to index.html. This allows the users to access the application.
4. **Build Your React Application**: Build your React application using npm run build or yarn build.
5. **Upload Build Files to S3:** Upload the contents of the build directory to your S3 bucket.
6. **Create a CloudFront Distribution**: Search for CloudFront in the AWS console, and then create a new distribution.
7. **Configure CloudFront:** Configure CloudFront by setting your S3 bucket as the origin, and configuring your domain name.
8. **Deploy:** Once the CloudFront distribution is created, the changes to your application will automatically be updated as you add new files to the S3 bucket.

Using AWS can be much more complex than using Vercel or Netlify, but you have much more control over how your application is configured. If your application requires complex infrastructure or security requirements, AWS will often be the best platform to pick.

Choosing The Right Platform

- **Vercel:** Vercel is often the best platform if you want to deploy your frontend application very quickly and easily. It handles a lot of the configuration automatically, which makes it a great choice for quickly deploying your applications.
- **Netlify:** Netlify is also an excellent choice that is also very easy to use, and has all the tools and features that most frontend developers would require.
- **AWS**: AWS provides an unmatched amount of flexibility, scalability, and configurability, but it is also more complex, and requires more understanding to configure.

Personal Insight

When I first started deploying React applications, I always found the deployment process tedious and complicated. I would have to manually build my applications, and then upload the files to the server. After discovering tools like Vercel and Netlify, I found that my life as a developer became much easier. Nowadays, I often prefer Vercel because its ease of use, but I will often reach for AWS if my application has specific requirements.

Key Takeaways:

- Vercel is an excellent option for deploying React applications, with its zero configuration approach, and automatic updates.
- Netlify is also a popular platform that provides most of the functionality that Vercel provides, with a slightly steeper learning curve, but also providing more configuration options.
- AWS provides a very flexible, and scalable solution for hosting any application, but often comes with the price of being more difficult to setup and configure.
- The best platform to pick, will depend on your unique needs, and the specific requirements of your project.

By understanding the differences between Vercel, Netlify, and AWS, you'll be equipped to choose the right platform for your React applications, ensuring that they are deployed efficiently and reliably. This is a key part of the development process that is often overlooked.

10.2 SETTING UP CI/CD PIPELINES: AUTOMATING YOUR WORKFLOW

CI/CD (Continuous Integration/Continuous Deployment) pipelines are a set of practices that automate the process of building, testing, and deploying your applications. This automation can greatly reduce the chance of human errors, provide you with faster feedback loops, and allow for more frequent releases. Setting up a CI/CD pipeline is crucial for creating a smooth development process.

What is CI/CD?

- **Continuous Integration (CI):** This focuses on integrating code changes from multiple developers into a shared repository frequently. It involves steps such as building, linting, and testing, and ensures that code changes are compatible with other parts of the application.
- **Continuous Deployment (CD):** This automates the process of deploying code changes to a production environment. This can include different environments such as staging, and development, depending on your specific requirements.

Benefits of CI/CD

- **Automation**: Automates the process of building, testing, and deploying your applications.
- **Faster Releases**: Reduces the time it takes for new features or bug fixes to reach production.
- **Improved Code Quality:** Introduces automated checks to ensure that your code meets certain quality standards.
- **Reduced Errors**: Reduces human errors, as a lot of the manual steps are now automated, reducing the chance of deployment errors.

Setting up a Basic CI/CD Pipeline with GitHub Actions

GitHub Actions is a popular and powerful service that can be used to automate your CI/CD pipelines. It is often used by developers that are using GitHub as their code repository, because it is seamlessly integrated into the GitHub ecosystem.

Let's set up a basic CI/CD pipeline using GitHub Actions, where we are going to be deploying our React application to Vercel.

1. **Create a Workflow File:** First, you will need to create a directory named .github/workflows in the root of your Git repository. Inside that directory, create a file named deploy.yml.
2. **Define the Workflow**: Open the deploy.yml and paste in the following code:

```yaml
name: CI/CD Pipeline
on:
  push:
    branches:
      - main
jobs:
  deploy:
    runs-on: ubuntu-latest
    steps:
      - name: Checkout code
        uses: actions/checkout@v3
      - name: Setup Node.js
        uses: actions/setup-node@v3
        with:
          node-version: 18
      - name: Install dependencies
        run: npm ci
      - name: Build
        run: npm run build
      - name: Deploy to Vercel
        uses: amondnet/vercel-action@v20
        with:
          vercel-token: ${{ secrets.VERCEL_TOKEN }}
          vercel-org-id: ${{ secrets.VERCEL_ORG_ID }}
          vercel-project-id: ${{ secrets.VERCEL_PROJECT_ID }}
```

Here's a breakdown of what each part of this file is doing:

- name: CI/CD Pipeline: This defines the name of our workflow, and will be shown in our github actions tab.
- on: push: This defines when the workflow should be triggered. In our case, we are going to be running the workflow on any push event to the main branch.
- jobs: deploy: This will define the jobs that are running in our workflow.
- runs-on: ubuntu-latest: This defines which server the workflow should run on. In our case we are running it on the latest version of ubuntu.
- steps: These are the steps that will run in the workflow.
  - **actions/checkout@v3**: This will checkout your code so that you can use it in your workflow.

- o **actions/setup-node@v3**: This step will install the specified node version, so that we can build our application.
- o npm ci: This will install all of your dependencies based on your package-lock.json, or yarn.lock file.
- o npm run build: This will build our react application.
- o **amondnet/vercel-action@v20**: This will deploy our application to vercel using the vercel action. You will need to provide the Vercel tokens using GitHub secrets, which we will explain later.

1. **Add Vercel Tokens to GitHub Secrets:** To deploy to Vercel, you will need to add the Vercel tokens to your repository's secrets. To do this navigate to your repository's settings, and then select "Secrets and variables", and click "Actions".
   - o You will need to create the following three secrets: VERCEL_TOKEN, VERCEL_ORG_ID, and VERCEL_PROJECT_ID.
     - The Vercel token can be created in Vercel's settings.
     - The Vercel Org ID can be found in Vercel's settings.
     - The Vercel Project ID can be found in the settings of your project.
2. **Commit and Push**: Now you will commit and push your changes to the main branch. This will automatically trigger the GitHub actions workflow, and it will deploy your application to Vercel, if everything is configured correctly.

You can see the workflow in action by navigating to the "Actions" tab in your GitHub repository, which you can use to track the progress of the builds.

CI/CD with Netlify

Netlify also provides a built-in CI/CD system that you can configure in your Netlify settings. To enable it you can connect your Git repository to Netlify, and it will automatically build and deploy your code on each push.

CI/CD with AWS

If you are hosting your application on AWS, then you can use AWS CodePipeline to set up your CI/CD workflow. This process will be more complex, but it will also be more configurable. This is beyond the scope of this chapter, but if you are interested, I would encourage you to look into the documentation of how to implement CI/CD using AWS CodePipeline.

Practical Implementation: Adding Tests to Your CI/CD Pipeline

Let's add a testing step to our current GitHub Actions workflow, to make sure our code passes all of our tests before we deploy it:

```
name: CI/CD Pipeline
on:
  push:
    branches:
      - main
jobs:
  deploy:
    runs-on: ubuntu-latest
    steps:
      - name: Checkout code
        uses: actions/checkout@v3
      - name: Setup Node.js
        uses: actions/setup-node@v3
        with:
          node-version: 18
      - name: Install dependencies
        run: npm ci
      - name: Run tests
        run: npm run test
      - name: Build
        run: npm run build
      - name: Deploy to Vercel
        uses: amondnet/vercel-action@v20
        with:
          vercel-token: ${{ secrets.VERCEL_TOKEN }}
          vercel-org-id: ${{ secrets.VERCEL_ORG_ID }}
          vercel-project-id: ${{ secrets.VERCEL_PROJECT_ID }}
```

Here, we have introduced a new step before building our application, where we are running our tests using npm run test. If all of our tests do not pass, then the pipeline will fail and not deploy the application to Vercel. This will help to make sure that only tests that have passed are deployed to production.

Personal Insight

When I first started developing React applications, I didn't know how valuable CI/CD pipelines were, and I was always deploying my applications manually, which was not only time consuming, but it was also very error prone. When I started implementing CI/CD, my development workflow improved drastically, and I was able to ship features faster, and also catch bugs before they reached production. Now, I will not develop an application without CI/CD.

Key Takeaways:

- CI/CD (Continuous Integration/Continuous Deployment) pipelines automate the process of building, testing, and deploying applications.
- GitHub Actions can be used to easily implement CI/CD workflows.
- You can also use CI/CD workflows with Netlify, or AWS CodePipeline.
- It is very important to include automated testing in your CI/CD pipeline to ensure that you are catching bugs before they are deployed to production.

By understanding how to setup CI/CD pipelines, you'll be able to streamline your development process, reduce errors, and deploy your applications with confidence. This is a key component of any modern web application.

Okay, let's explore the crucial aspects of performance monitoring and error tracking for React applications. Once your app is deployed, it's vital to understand how it's performing and to catch any errors that may arise. We'll examine various tools and strategies to help you keep your application running smoothly and reliably.

10.3 PERFORMANCE MONITORING AND ERROR TRACKING: KEEPING YOUR APP HEALTHY

Performance monitoring and error tracking are essential for ensuring that your React applications are not only functional, but also providing a good user experience. Without proper monitoring and tracking, you may not be able to catch bugs or performance issues until it is too late. By implementing the right tools and processes, you will be able to keep your application healthy, and responsive to your user's needs.

Performance Monitoring: Understanding How Your App Performs

Performance monitoring involves tracking key metrics of your application to see how it is performing. These metrics can be used to identify slow parts of your code, and help you to optimize them.

There are many tools you can use to monitor the performance of your website, but we will be covering Google Analytics and Lighthouse, as these are some of the most popular tools that developers often use.

Google Analytics: User Behavior and Traffic Analysis

Google Analytics is a free web analytics service that allows you to track how users interact with your website. It provides many valuable metrics, that can be used to identify usage patterns, and also to understand potential bottlenecks in your application.

Here are some key benefits of Google Analytics:

- **Traffic Analysis:** Track the amount of users visiting your site, as well as the sources of the traffic.
- **User Behavior**: Understand how users are navigating your application, the pages they are visiting, how long they are on each page, and other metrics to understand how users interact with your application.
- **Conversion Tracking**: Track conversion goals, such as form submissions or product purchases, and understand where your users are dropping off.

Practical Implementation: Setting up Google Analytics

1. **Create a Google Analytics Account:** Go to Google Analytics and create a new account if you don't have one.
2. **Create a Property:** Create a new property for your React application, and obtain the tracking ID.
3. **Install the Google Analytics Library:** Install the react-ga4 library using the command npm install react-ga4
4. **Initialize Google Analytics:** In your application, you will initialize Google Analytics with your tracking ID:

```
import React from 'react';
import ReactGA from "react-ga4";

function App(){
    ReactGA.initialize("YOUR_TRACKING_ID");
    ReactGA.send( { hitType: "pageview", page:
window.location.pathname });
    return (
        <h1>My React Application</h1>
    )
}
export default App;
```

You will have to use your tracking ID in place of "YOUR_TRACKING_ID". This will now track all of the pages that the users visit. You can then use the Google Analytics dashboard to view your data.

Lighthouse: Website Performance and Accessibility

Lighthouse is an open-source tool from Google, which you can access by right-clicking and selecting "Inspect" on your webpage, and then going to the "Lighthouse" tab. It provides audits on your website, looking at performance, accessibility, best practices, and SEO.

Here are some key benefits of using Lighthouse:

- **Performance Metrics**: Provides important metrics such as: First Contentful Paint (FCP), Largest Contentful Paint (LCP), and Cumulative Layout Shift (CLS), which can be used to measure the performance of your website.
- **Optimization Suggestions**: Provides recommendations and actionable steps you can take to improve your website.
- **Accessibility Testing**: Helps you identify areas of your application that may not be accessible to all of your users.
- **SEO Checks:** Helps you improve your search engine ranking by identifying areas to improve SEO.

To use lighthouse, all you need to do is open up your developer tools, and select the Lighthouse tab, and then click "Analyze page load".

Error Tracking: Catching Bugs Before Your Users

Error tracking involves collecting information about errors that occur in your application, so that you can then debug the issue and improve the experience of your users. This allows you to catch bugs before they affect your users.

There are many different error tracking tools out there, but we will be covering Sentry and Bugsnag, as these are two of the most popular choices for React developers.

Sentry: Comprehensive Error Tracking

Sentry is an error tracking service that helps you monitor your application and track errors, and will also show you the exact place in the code where the error happened. It also provides a lot of integrations with other services, and has a very user friendly dashboard to view all of your errors.

Key features of Sentry:

- **Error Reporting**: Capture all errors that occur in your frontend and backend.
- **Detailed Context**: Provides valuable context about the errors, such as the browser, operating system, user actions, and more.
- **Alerts:** Allows you to setup alerts, so that you are notified whenever a new error has occurred.
- **Performance Monitoring:** Also has the ability to monitor the performance of your application.

Setting up Sentry in React

1. **Create a Sentry Account:** Go to Sentry's website and create a new account.
2. **Create a New Project**: After creating your account, create a new project for your application, and copy the DSN key that is provided.
3. **Install the Sentry SDK**: Install the Sentry SDK using npm install @sentry/react @sentry/tracing.
4. **Initialize Sentry**: In your application, initialize Sentry:

```
import React from 'react';
import * as Sentry from "@sentry/react";
import { BrowserTracing } from "@sentry/tracing";

Sentry.init({
  dsn: "YOUR_SENTRY_DSN",
  integrations: [new BrowserTracing()],
  tracesSampleRate: 1.0,
});
function App(){
    return (
        <h1>My React Application</h1>
    )
}
export default App;
```

Make sure you use your DSN key instead of "YOUR_SENTRY_DSN". This will automatically capture all errors in your application, and you can view them in the Sentry dashboard.

Bugsnag: A Robust Alternative

Bugsnag is another popular error tracking service, that is very similar to Sentry, and often used as an alternative to Sentry. It also provides a robust set of tools to track errors in your application, and to help you debug issues.

Key features of Bugsnag:

- **Error Capture**: Captures and reports all the errors that happen in your application.
- **Detailed Error Reporting**: Provides very detailed reports about the errors, such as the specific lines of code where the errors occurred, as well as other information.
- **Filtering and Grouping**: Allows you to filter and group errors by different attributes, making it easier to find the most relevant errors.

Setting up Bugsnag in React

1. **Create a Bugsnag Account**: Navigate to Bugsnag's website and create a new account.
2. **Create a Project**: Create a new project, and obtain the API key.
3. **Install Bugsnag**: Install the Bugsnag SDK using npm install @bugsnag/js @bugsnag/plugin-react.
4. **Initialize Bugsnag**: In your application, initialize Bugsnag:

```
import React from 'react';
import Bugsnag from '@bugsnag/js';
import BugsnagPluginReact from '@bugsnag/plugin-react';

Bugsnag.start({
    apiKey: 'YOUR_BUGSNAG_API_KEY',
    plugins: [new BugsnagPluginReact()],
});
function App() {
    return (
       <h1>My React Application</h1>
    );
}
export default App;
```

Make sure you replace "YOUR_BUGSNAG_API_KEY" with your Bugsnag API key. Just like Sentry, this will capture errors and show them in the Bugsnag dashboard.

Choosing Between Sentry and Bugsnag

Both Sentry and Bugsnag are excellent error tracking services, and often it depends on personal preference on which one you choose. I prefer Sentry due to its integrations with other services, as well as its robust features, but you should also explore Bugsnag, and find the tool that best suits your needs.

Personal Insight

When I first started developing applications, I didn't have a robust way to track errors in production, and I often only discovered bugs when my users would report them. After discovering Sentry and Bugsnag, I realized how crucial error tracking was, and how it can greatly improve your workflow. I always recommend using a proper error tracking tool in all of your applications.

Key Takeaways:

- Performance monitoring tools such as Google Analytics and Lighthouse, are used to identify slow parts of your application, and also helps you to analyze user behavior.
- Error tracking tools, such as Sentry and Bugsnag, can be used to capture and analyze errors that happen in your application, so that you can debug the issues before they affect your users.
- Both performance monitoring and error tracking are crucial for ensuring the reliability and robustness of your applications.

By implementing proper performance monitoring and error tracking, you will be able to ensure that your React applications are not only high-performing, but also provide a great experience for your end users. These are all skills that you will need to develop when building any React application.

10.4 BEST PRACTICES FOR PRODUCTION-READY REACT APPS: A HOLISTIC APPROACH

Creating a production-ready React application involves a lot more than just writing the code. It requires a deep understanding of performance optimization, testing strategies, deployment best practices, and also a good understanding of your application and its potential bottlenecks. Let's explore some key aspects that you should consider.

Performance Optimization: Ensuring Speed and Efficiency

Performance optimization is a continuous process and is often a critical part of building a good React application. This is because slow applications will cause a very bad user experience, and are often ignored by end users.

Here are some best practices to keep in mind:

- **Code Splitting and Lazy Loading:** Use code splitting to divide your application into smaller chunks that are loaded on demand, rather than loading everything upfront. Use React's lazy function, in combination with Suspense, to only load components when they are needed.
- **Memoization:** Utilize useMemo and useCallback to prevent expensive calculations, and to also prevent functions from being re-created on every render. This helps to prevent unnecessary re-renders of your components.
- **Image Optimization:** Optimize your images by compressing them, and resizing them to be appropriate for the size they will be displayed. You should also use the correct image formats. For images that are less complex you should use WebP, for pictures you should use JPG, and for things with transparency you should use PNG.
- **Minification:** Use tools such as Webpack, or Terser to minify your code, which will reduce its size.
- **Compression:** Compress your code using Gzip, or Brotli, which further reduces its size, and improves the load times of your application.
- **Tree Shaking**: Use tree shaking, to remove dead code. This will remove any code that is not being used, reducing the overall size of your code.

Testing: Ensuring Reliability and Robustness

Testing is an essential part of any software application, and your React application is no exception. Having a good testing strategy, using unit, integration, and end to end testing is an essential part of creating a high quality application.

Here are some key concepts to keep in mind:

- **Unit Tests**: Write unit tests for individual components and functions, to make sure that they are working as expected. This will give you the flexibility to refactor your code, knowing that if you introduce any errors you will catch them with the unit tests.
- **Component and Integration Tests**: Use component and integration tests to make sure that the different parts of your application are working together, often mocking out external dependencies.

- **End to End Tests:** Use end to end tests to test your application from the user's perspective, to make sure that your application is working correctly from the user's perspective.

Deployment: Choosing the Right Platform

Your deployment strategy has a large impact on your application's performance, and choosing a good platform that is fit for your needs is essential.

- **Vercel**: Use Vercel if you want an easy to use deployment platform, and if you do not require granular control.
- **Netlify**: Netlify is another popular choice that also provides a very easy way to deploy React applications, but is more versatile and also has more configuration options.
- **AWS**: Use AWS if you require a very flexible, and scalable solution, but are also okay with the added complexity of configuring your AWS setup.

CI/CD Pipelines: Automation for Faster Releases

CI/CD (Continuous Integration and Continuous Deployment) pipelines automate the process of building, testing, and deploying your application. This helps to make sure that you deploy your application as reliably as possible, without having to manually deploy your application.

- **GitHub Actions**: GitHub Actions can be used to implement CI/CD workflows for your repository on GitHub. This is an excellent option if you use GitHub as your code repository.
- **Netlify or Vercel**: Both Netlify and Vercel provide CI/CD pipelines that are often enabled by default.
- **AWS CodePipeline**: AWS CodePipeline provides a configurable CI/CD solution for AWS.

Error Tracking: Monitoring Your Application

Error tracking is a way of capturing and logging any errors that occur in your application. This will help you identify the areas where your code is failing. It is not enough to just test your code, but you should also track your application to make sure that everything is working as expected in production.

- **Sentry:** Sentry is a popular error tracking service that provides a very detailed view of all the errors that happen in your code, and also provides details about the environment the error occurred.

- **Bugsnag:** Bugsnag is another excellent alternative to Sentry, that provides similar functionality.

Accessibility: Ensuring Inclusivity

Accessibility is ensuring that your application is usable by everyone, including people with disabilities. There are many tools that you can use to improve the accessibility of your application, such as using proper semantic HTML, ensuring that you have a good color contrast, and also using proper ARIA labels on interactive elements.

Security: Protecting Your Users and Your Application

Implementing good security practices is an essential part of building a production ready application. This could include properly sanitizing user inputs, using secure protocols such as HTTPS, and protecting against cross-site scripting.

Environment Variables

Environment variables are used to store configuration variables that are needed for your application. They are stored outside of your code, and will change based on the environment that your application is running on. You should never hard code values such as API keys, but instead you should store them in environment variables.

Documentation: Providing Clarity

Providing good documentation will help developers that are working on your project in the future. You should always document your code, and make it easy for new developers to understand how all the different parts of the application works.

Performance Monitoring:

Use tools like Google Analytics, and Lighthouse to test your application for performance bottlenecks, and also to monitor the real world performance of your application.

Personal Insight

When I first started building React applications, I was often focused on just making things work, and didn't really pay attention to the aspects of building production ready applications. After spending some time working in the industry, I realized that it is also essential to focus on all of these other things, such as performance, security, testing, accessibility, and maintainability, to build truly robust and high quality applications. These are all techniques that I now incorporate into all of the applications that I build.

Key Takeaways:

- Performance optimization should always be a consideration when developing a React application, and there are many techniques you can use to make your application perform faster.
- Testing is essential for making sure that your application is reliable, and you should have a good testing strategy.
- Your deployment strategy will have a large impact on your application, so you should carefully pick the platform that is right for your needs.
- Having a CI/CD pipeline will ensure that your code is deployed reliably and quickly.
- You should use tools such as Sentry or Bugsnag to track errors that occur in production.
- You should always keep accessibility, and security in mind, and make sure that your application is usable by as many people as possible.

By using all of the techniques that we have learned in this chapter, you will be able to create production ready applications that perform well, are reliable, and easy to maintain. These are all the aspects that you will need to consider when building a serious React application.

CHAPTER 11: THE FUTURE OF REACT AND NEXT STEPS

This chapter marks the end of our comprehensive guide through React, but it is also the beginning of your journey as a React developer. This chapter will outline the roadmap of React, discuss how to expand your skills using Next.js, and also discuss how to build a career as a React developer. Let's explore what's next!

11.1 UPCOMING FEATURES AND REACT ROADMAP: PEEKING INTO THE FUTURE

React is a constantly evolving library, and the React team is always working on new features, performance improvements, and also improvements to the developer experience. Staying informed about the React roadmap is important for any React developer, so that you can be prepared for new features, and ensure that your skills remain up to date.

Key Areas of Focus

The React team is focusing on several areas, that aim to enhance the user experience, as well as provide better developer tools.

- **React Server Components (RSCs):** This is a new way to render components on the server. Unlike server-side rendering (SSR) where the entire page is rendered on the server, RSCs allows for some of your component code to run on the server, while other parts of the code will run on the client. These components can fetch data from the server without having to send a request from the client, reducing the load on the client and also resulting in faster load times.
- **Data Fetching Improvements:** There is a big focus on improving the different ways that React fetches data. This includes improving the current APIs such as useEffect, as well as providing new components that can be used to handle data fetching.
- **Concurrency:** The React team is also focusing on concurrency, which aims to improve the way that React handles rendering. This will make React applications more performant and responsive.
- **Ecosystem Growth:** This includes improving the React ecosystem, by adding new tools, libraries, and integrations with other services.

- **Developer Experience**: React is also focusing on providing tools to improve the overall developer experience, such as more descriptive errors, as well as performance improvements to its core rendering mechanisms.

React Server Components (RSCs): A New Paradigm

React Server Components (RSCs) are the latest way of building React applications. This is a feature that is built on top of server side rendering (SSR). With RSCs, different components in your application can render on the server, while other components can render on the client side.

Here's how it works:

- **Server-Side Rendering:** Some components can run on the server, allowing them to fetch data, and then send the resulting HTML to the client.
- **Client-Side Rendering:** Other components will still be running on the client, and will handle user interactions.
- **Improved Performance**: This can greatly improve initial load times, as well as improve the performance of your application, because some of the work is being done on the server.
- **Data Fetching:** Allows components to fetch data from the server, without the overhead of a separate API call from the client.

You can see this by navigating to a Next.js application, and creating a file under the pages directory, such as pages/my-page.js.

```
import React from 'react';
async function getData() {
  // This is a server function, and will not be included in your
client code.
    const response = await
fetch("https://jsonplaceholder.typicode.com/todos/1");
  const data = await response.json();
  return data;
}
export default async function MyPage() {
    const data = await getData();
    return (
        <div>
          <h1>My page</h1>
          <p>Title: {data.title}</p>
        </div>
    );
}
```

Here we are defining an async component in Next.js, that fetches data on the server side, which you can see is not downloaded to the client side. This allows for a much faster initial page load. React server components can also be added inside of client components using the 'use client'; directive. This tells React that this component will be running on the client side, and will not be rendered on the server.

Data Fetching Improvements: Streamlining Data Retrieval

The React team is also working on improving the data fetching mechanisms in React. This includes making the current APIs, such as useEffect, more flexible, as well as providing new built-in ways of fetching data. This often includes providing better support for caching data, data deduplication, and automatic invalidation of cached data.

Concurrency: Making React More Responsive

Concurrency is another area of focus for the React team. Concurrency aims to improve the way that React handles rendering, which allows for better performance, and a much smoother user experience.

Staying Updated

To stay informed about the future of React, here are a few strategies you should follow:

- **Official React Blog:** The official React blog is the main source for announcements, new features, and changes, and is often the first place you will hear about them.
- **React Documentation:** The React documentation is constantly being updated to reflect the latest changes, and also provides practical examples on how to implement them.
- **React GitHub Repository:** The React GitHub repository is where the code for React is being developed. By keeping up to date on what's happening in the repository, you can get a sense of what the React team is working on.
- **React Community:** The React community is often the first people to try out all the new features. Following other developers will help you see the different ways that developers are implementing these new changes in their applications.
- **React Conferences:** Attending conferences will help you stay updated, and also network with other developers.

Personal Insight

I remember when I first started using React, I was often confused by all the different ways that people were fetching data. The React team seems to be focusing on providing solutions to problems that many React developers are facing. I am very excited to see how React Server Components, and the data fetching changes will improve the way that we all develop React applications.

Key Takeaways:

- The React team is focusing on React Server Components (RSCs), data fetching improvements, concurrency, ecosystem growth, and improving the developer experience.
- React Server Components (RSCs) are a new way of building react applications, that will make React apps more performant, and reduce the complexity of fetching data.
- To stay updated you should follow the official React blog, documentation, as well as follow the open source React GitHub repository. You should also be involved in the community to learn new things, and to see what other developers are building.

By staying informed about the React roadmap, you'll be well-prepared for the future of React development. These are the core concepts that you will need to understand to build modern React applications.

11.2 LEARNING NEXT.JS FOR FULL-STACK DEVELOPMENT: EXPANDING YOUR REACT SKILLS

While React excels as a frontend library for building user interfaces, it often requires additional tools and libraries to handle backend logic, data fetching, routing, and server-side rendering (SSR). This is where Next.js steps in, providing a complete framework that builds on top of React and allows you to build full-stack applications with a more streamlined and simplified developer experience. For a React developer, learning Next.js is one of the best ways to expand your skills, and also create more robust applications.

Why Learn Next.js?

Next.js offers a number of key features:

- **Server-Side Rendering (SSR):** Next.js has built-in support for server-side rendering, which improves the initial load time, SEO, and accessibility of your application.
- **Static Site Generation (SSG):** You can also use SSG for pages that don't change very often, which will generate your HTML files at build time, for blazing fast page loads.
- **API Routes:** It provides an easy way to create backend APIs, by using serverless functions that can be written in the /pages/api directory.
- **File-System Routing:** Uses a file system based routing system, which makes it much easier to create new pages in your application.
- **Developer Experience:** It provides a very smooth and easy to use developer experience, with many built in features, such as hot reloading.
- **Large Community:** Next.js has a very large and active community, which provides a vast amount of learning resources.

Key Concepts of Next.js

Before we start implementing code, let's explore some of the core concepts of Next.js:

- **Pages Directory:** The pages directory is where you will create all of your routes. Any files that you put in this directory will be automatically created as a route, and will be accessible via its file name. For example if you create a file called pages/about.js, it will automatically be rendered at the /about route.
- **Components:** Just like React, you can create reusable components, that will be used in the pages you build.
- **Data Fetching:** Next.js provides getStaticProps for static site generation, and getServerSideProps for server side rendering. These functions are used to fetch data before the component is rendered.
- **API Routes:** Any file you create inside of the pages/api directory, will automatically be turned into an API endpoint.
- **Layouts**: Next.js allows you to create reusable layouts, that wrap your pages, using the _app.js file.

Practical Implementation: Building a Simple Blog

Let's build a simple blog to see how to use Next.js in a real application:

1. **Create a New Next.js Application:** Start by creating a new Next.js application:

```
    npx create-next-app my-blog
cd my-blog
npm run dev
```

2. **Create the Home Page**: Open up the pages/index.js file and replace its content:

```
    import React from 'react';
function Home(){
    return (
        <div>
         <h1>Welcome to my Blog</h1>
     </div>
 )
}
export default Home;
```

Create a Blog Post Page: Create a new file inside of the pages directory called pages/blog/[slug].js:
```
    import React from 'react';
export async function getStaticPaths(){
    return {
        paths: [
            { params: { slug: 'post-1' } },
            { params: { slug: 'post-2' } },
        ],
      fallback: false
    }
}
export async function getStaticProps({ params }){
    const slug = params.slug;
   const post = {
      slug: slug,
      title: `Blog Post ${slug}`,
      content: `This is the content of blog post ${slug}`,
    }
    return {
       props: {
          post
        }
     }
}
function BlogPost({ post }){
    return (
        <div>
          <h1>{post.title}</h1>
          <p>{post.content}</p>
      </div>
    );
```

```
}
export default BlogPost;
```

Here's what's happening:

- **getStaticPaths:** This function is used when you are using SSG. This
  is where you define all of the routes that are available to the user.
- **getStaticProps:** This function is called at build time. Here we are
  getting the slug from the route parameters and then creating our blog
  post object, and passing it down as a prop.
- **BlogPost Component:** This is the component that renders the data
  from the getStaticProps function.

3. **Create a Blog Index Page:** Create a new file inside of the pages directory
   called pages/blog/index.js:

```
import React from 'react';
import Link from 'next/link';
function BlogIndex(){
  const posts = [
      { slug: 'post-1', title: 'Blog Post 1' },
      { slug: 'post-2', title: 'Blog Post 2' },
  ]
return (
    <div>
        <h1>Blog Posts</h1>
        <ul>
          {posts.map(post => (
              <li key={post.slug}>
                <Link
href={`/blog/${post.slug}`}>{post.title}</Link>
              </li>
          ))}
        </ul>
    </div>
);
}
export default BlogIndex;
```

Here's what's happening:

- We have created a component that displays a list of blog posts.
- We are using the Link component from Next.js to create links to the
  blog posts. The href property specifies where the link should navigate
  to.

4. **Create a Navigation Component:** Create a new file inside the components directory called components/Nav.js:

```
import Link from "next/link";
import React from "react";
function Nav() {
    return (
      <nav>
        <ul>
          <li><Link href="/">Home</Link></li>
            <li><Link href="/blog">Blog</Link></li>
        </ul>
      </nav>
    );
}
export default Nav;
```

- Here we are creating a component that shows all of our links to our pages.

1. **Create a Layout Component:** Create a new file called pages/_app.js:

```
import React from 'react';
import Nav from "../components/Nav";
function MyApp({ Component, pageProps }){
  return (
        <div>
            <Nav />
            <Component {...pageProps} />
        </div>
    )
}
export default MyApp;
```

- Here, we are creating a layout component that will be used to render our navigation bar on all of our pages.
- The Component prop will be the page that we want to render, and the pageProps are all the props that are passed down to that component.

Now when you run the application using npm run dev you can see a simple blog that uses server side rendering, as well as static site generation.

Learning Resources

- **Next.js Documentation:** The official documentation is the best source for learning about Next.js, and should be your first stop.
- **Next.js Learn Website:** The official learn website, provides tutorials, and courses that are a great place to start learning.
- **Online Courses:** There are many great courses online on platforms such as Udemy, Coursera, and Skillshare.
- **Blog Posts and Tutorials:** There are also many blog posts, and tutorials created by other developers on the internet, that you can use as a reference.

Personal Insight

When I first started learning Next.js, I was amazed at how much it improved the developer experience. The file system routing, automatic SSR and SSG, and the ability to create serverless functions drastically improved my workflow. I highly recommend that any React developer also looks into Next.js.

Key Takeaways:

- Next.js is a framework that builds on top of React, that allows you to create full stack applications.
- Next.js provides server side rendering (SSR), and static site generation (SSG), which drastically improves the performance of your application.
- Next.js also provides a file system based routing, as well as API routes for you to create your backend endpoints.
- You can also use custom layouts to style your pages consistently.

By learning Next.js you will greatly improve your skills as a developer, and also allow you to create full stack React applications. Next.js is the recommended framework by many developers and I would highly encourage you to explore it.

11.3 BUILDING A CAREER AS A REACT DEVELOPER: A PRACTICAL ROADMAP

The demand for React developers is very high, making it a very viable and exciting career path. However, simply learning React is not enough. To be successful, you need a combination of technical skills, a great portfolio, networking abilities, and also soft skills. Let's explore what you can do to enhance your chances of building a successful career.

Building a Strong Portfolio: Showcasing Your Skills

A strong portfolio is the most essential part of finding jobs as a developer. It allows you to showcase your skills, your experience, and the types of projects that you enjoy working on. Employers will often look at your portfolio to assess your technical skills, so it is very important that you have a well-built and easy to navigate portfolio.

Here are some tips for building a strong portfolio:

- **Variety of Projects:** Showcase a wide range of projects to demonstrate your versatility. Include different types of applications, such as e-commerce sites, landing pages, and data visualization tools.
- **Clean and Organized Code**: Always write clean and organized code, so that employers can understand your code.
- **Proper Documentation:** Document your code, so that other developers can understand the parts that you have built.
- **Responsive Designs:** Ensure that your projects are responsive and accessible on different screen sizes and devices.
- **Focus on User Experience**: Always focus on creating a good user experience, so that users can easily use your applications.
- **Deploy Your Portfolio:** Make sure that you host your portfolio using a reliable platform like Vercel, Netlify, or AWS.

Practical Implementation: Creating a Portfolio Website

Let's look at the steps required to create a portfolio website:

1. **Choose a Hosting Platform**: Choose a hosting platform such as Vercel or Netlify.
2. **Create a New React Application**: You can either build your portfolio website using create-react-app, or using a full stack framework such as Next.js.
3. **Design Your Portfolio**: Design a portfolio that is easy to navigate, and also allows you to showcase your projects. Include sections such as:
   - **Home:** Where you introduce yourself and showcase your skills.
   - **Projects:** Where you show all the different projects that you have built.
   - **About:** Where you talk about your experience, and your background.
   - **Contact:** Where you include your contact information, and a contact form, so that people can reach out to you.
   - **Blog (Optional):** A blog is also a great way to showcase your skills, by writing about technologies that you are learning, or interesting topics that you are exploring.

4. **Deploy Your Portfolio:** Make sure you deploy your portfolio to one of the hosting providers that we previously discussed.

Contributing to Open Source: Learning and Collaboration

Contributing to open source projects is a great way to not only learn from other developers, but also to showcase your skills and your ability to collaborate with other developers. It is also a very valuable way to get familiar with production level code.

Here are some tips for contributing to open source projects:

- **Pick Projects That Align With Your Interests**: Pick a project that is of interest to you. You are more likely to keep contributing if you are enjoying the project.
- **Start Small**: Start with small, well defined tasks, such as fixing typos, adding documentation, or fixing small bugs.
- **Follow the Guidelines**: Make sure to read the contribution guidelines of the project, and that you are following the development standards and practices of the project.
- **Be Active in the Community:** Be active in the project's community by asking questions, and helping other developers.

Networking: Building Relationships

Networking is a great way to build relationships with other developers, and also to find new opportunities in the industry.

Here are a few ways that you can build your network:

- **Attend Meetups:** Attend local meetups, where you will meet other developers, and learn more about what other people in the industry are working on.
- **Conferences**: Attend conferences, where you can hear from industry experts, and also network with other developers.
- **Online Communities:** Participate in online communities, such as online forums, Slack channels, and Discord groups, to also meet new people.
- **Social Media:** Follow other developers on social media such as X (formerly Twitter), LinkedIn, and Github, to stay updated with their work.

Continuous Learning: Staying Ahead of the Curve

The React ecosystem is constantly evolving, so it is very important to continuously learn new things, and also explore new libraries and frameworks.

Here are some tips for staying up to date:

- **Follow Blogs:** Follow blogs from industry leaders, and the official React blog.
- **Podcasts:** Listen to podcasts, such as The React Podcast, to also hear about the new developments in the React community.
- **Documentation:** Follow the React, and Next.js documentation, to learn about the new features and updates to those frameworks.
- **Online Courses:** Keep learning by taking courses in different online platforms such as Udemy, Coursera, or Skillshare.

Soft Skills: Effective Communication

While technical skills are very important, soft skills are just as crucial for a successful career. Having soft skills such as communication, teamwork, and problem solving are what will help you succeed in the industry.

Here are some areas you can focus on:

- **Communication**: You should be able to clearly communicate your ideas to other people, whether it is in writing, or verbally.
- **Teamwork:** You should be able to collaborate with other developers, and also contribute to a common goal.
- **Problem Solving:** You should have the ability to analyze a problem, and then provide a solution.
- **Adaptability:** The ability to adapt to new technologies and changing circumstances is often very important when building software.

Personal Insight

When I first started my career, I was often focused on only building my technical skills, and did not pay attention to soft skills, or networking. After some time, I realized how important networking, and soft skills are to be successful. I also realized that I need to continue to learn to make sure my skills remain up to date. This is why I highly encourage you to focus on continuous learning, and all of the other skills, and suggestions outlined here.

Key Takeaways:

- Building a strong portfolio is crucial for showcasing your skills, and finding new opportunities.
- Contributing to open source is a great way to collaborate with other developers, and to learn from experienced developers.
- Networking helps you build relationships with other developers, and also expand your career opportunities.
- You must have a focus on continuous learning, as the tech industry is always evolving.
- You must have strong soft skills, such as communication and teamwork, to be successful.

By focusing on these aspects, you'll be well-prepared to build a successful and rewarding career as a React developer. This is a marathon, and not a sprint, and it will take time and effort.

11.4 RECOMMENDED RESOURCES AND FURTHER LEARNING: A PATH TO MASTERY

As a React developer, you must always focus on continuous learning, as the React ecosystem is constantly evolving, and new tools and libraries are continuously being introduced. This section is dedicated to providing you with the resources to help you learn, grow, and enhance your skills as a React developer.

Official Documentation: The Core Reference

The official React documentation is the single best resource you can use when learning React, and it is also often the first place where new features are announced. The documentation is very well written, easy to understand, and also contains practical examples.

Here are the key reasons why you should rely on the official React documentation:

- **Accuracy**: The documentation is always kept up to date, and is the best source of truth for all the information.
- **Completeness:** It covers almost every aspect of React, from the core concepts, to advanced topics.
- **Examples:** The documentation contains many practical examples that you can use to understand the different features of React.
- **Updates:** The documentation is the first place to be updated when new features are released.

Next.js Documentation: Full-Stack Development

If you want to expand your React skills, then the official Next.js documentation is the next place you should go to. As we have discussed, Next.js provides a great way to create full stack applications, using React as its frontend, and also providing all the tooling to create your backend.

Key benefits of using the Next.js documentation:

- **Framework Specific Guidance**: It contains the most relevant and up to date information about the Next.js framework.
- **Full Stack Approach**: It covers topics that are related to the backend, as well as the frontend.
- **Practical Examples**: Provides many practical examples on how to implement different features of Next.js.

React Testing Library Documentation: User-Centric Testing

The React Testing Library is a library that encourages you to test components from the perspective of the end user, and this should be your primary way of testing your applications. The official documentation for the React Testing Library is the best place to learn about how to use the different features of the library, such as querying elements using getByRole, and simulating user events such as clicking and typing using fireEvent.

Blogs and Tutorials: Practical Insights

There are many great blogs and tutorials created by other developers, that often provide a much more hands-on way of learning. Here are some recommended blogs and authors that you can follow:

- **Kent C. Dodds Blog:** Kent C. Dodds is a popular author in the React community, and he writes about many different topics relating to React and JavaScript.
- **Dan Abramov's Blog:** Dan Abramov is one of the core members of the React team, and he writes about advanced React topics, as well as gives a good overview of the different technologies that are used in the React ecosystem.
- **Overreacted:** The blog of Dan Abramov, which provides many insights about the React library.
- **CSS-Tricks:** Although CSS-Tricks is primarily a blog about CSS, it also contains valuable content about React, and many other frontend topics.

Online Courses: Structured Learning

If you prefer a more structured approach to learning, there are many online courses that you can take:

- **Udemy**: Has a vast collection of courses on all different topics, including React, and Next.js.
- **Coursera:** Offers courses from top universities and organizations, and also provides a good learning path for web development.
- **Skillshare:** Skillshare offers a variety of courses that cover practical topics, and also focus on creative skills.
- **Frontend Masters:** Frontend Masters provides very high quality courses on a variety of frontend technologies.

Podcasts: Staying Updated on the Go

If you are busy, then podcasts are a great way to learn while commuting, going for a walk, or even while doing chores. Here are a few great podcasts that you can listen to:

- **The React Podcast:** Provides great interviews with people in the React community, as well as news about the latest updates to the React library.
- **Syntax.fm:** Provides information about web development, and provides a lot of practical information about HTML, CSS, and Javascript.

Open Source Projects: Learning by Doing

Open source projects are not only a great way to contribute to the community, but they are also a great way to learn by exploring real world codebases. By looking into how other developers implement their features, you will greatly enhance your skills as a developer.

Here are a few open source projects that you can explore:

- **React:** The official React repository contains a lot of valuable information, and code. By exploring the source code, you will get a better grasp of the library, and how it works under the hood.
- **Next.js:** The Next.js repository is another valuable resource, where you can see how the framework is implemented.
- **React Router:** This is a good library to explore if you are looking for ways to improve the routing in your application.

- **React Testing Library:** This library helps to test React applications in a user centric way, and is a great library to explore when you are learning how to test your application.

Practical Steps for Further Learning:

1. **Create a Learning Plan:** Define a clear learning plan, based on the topics that are interesting to you, as well as the skills that you are trying to learn.
2. **Set Goals:** Set realistic learning goals, and make sure that you are progressing at your own pace, without comparing yourself to others.
3. **Be Consistent:** Make sure you set a regular schedule where you can focus on your learning. It is important to be consistent, and dedicate time for your learning, even if it is a small amount of time.
4. **Practice:** The best way to learn is to practice. Make sure to build a variety of different applications, to solidify your understanding of the material.
5. **Apply What You Learn:** Every time you learn something new, make sure you try to incorporate it into your personal projects, to reinforce your learning.

Personal Insight

When I first started learning web development, I was often overwhelmed with the amount of things that I didn't know. I was often not sure where to start. Over time, I learned that it is important to pick a few resources, that you find that are valuable, and then focus on learning from those resources. I also learned how important it is to practice, and apply what you learned, as this is the best way to truly solidify your understanding.

Key Takeaways:

- The official documentation is always the best source of truth for learning about React, and also keeping up to date with the latest changes.
- Next.js is an excellent framework for building full stack applications, and its documentation is a must read for every React developer.
- Blogs and tutorials from other developers often provide very practical insights that can be very useful.
- Online courses are a good way to learn in a more structured way.
- Podcasts are a great way to stay updated with new changes and also new technologies.
- Open source projects are a good way to learn from real world examples, as well as to contribute to the community.

- Continuous learning is an essential part of being a successful React developer.

By utilizing these resources and following a structured learning approach, you'll be able to not only enhance your skills, but also be well-prepared for a successful and rewarding career as a React developer. Always continue to learn, experiment, and try new things.

www.ingramcontent.com/pod-product-compliance
Lightning Source LLC
LaVergne TN
LVHW081523050326
832903LV00025B/1600